WJEC
CBAC

HOSPITALITY
& CATERING
for GCSE Second Edition

Judy Gardiner

Jacqui Housley

HODDER
EDUCATION
AN HACHETTE UK COMPANY

Orders: please contact Bookpoint Ltd, 130 Milton Park, Abingdon, Oxon OX14 4SB.
Telephone: (44) 01235 827720. Fax: (44) 01235 400454. Lines are open from 9.00–5.00,
Monday to Saturday, with a 24 hour message answering service. You can also order
through our website www.hoddereducation.co.uk

If you have any comments to make about this, or any of our other titles, please send them to
educationenquiries@hodder.co.uk

British Library Cataloguing in Publication Data
A catalogue record for this title is available from the British Library

ISBN: 978 0 340 98682 0

First edition published 2007
This edition published 2009

Impression number   10 9 8 7 6 5
Year   2012 2011

Cover photo © ErickN – Fotolia.
Typeset by Pantek Arts Ltd., Maidstone, Kent.
Illustrations by Oxford Designers and Illustrators.
Printed in Dubai for Hodder Education, an Hachette UK Company, 338 Euston Road,
London NW1 3BH.

Contents

Contents

Introduction

This book has been revised to provide comprehensive support for the new specifications for GCSE Hospitality and Catering (from September 2009). It has been written to meet the needs of teachers and to support students studying GCSE Catering (single award), GCSE Hospitality (single award) or GCSE Hospitality and Catering (double award). It is also aimed at teachers and students interested in, or studying, all catering and hospitality courses.

The book provides a complete and unique source of information relevant to the study of Hospitality and Catering at GCSE level. It can be used as a 'one-stop' source of information for these courses. Students and teachers will find the contents easy to follow.

Students aiming to complete the single award in Catering will need to study Chapters 1 and 2.

Students aiming to complete the single award in Hospitality will need to study Chapters 3 and 4.

Students aiming to complete the double award in Hospitality and Catering will need to study all chapters (1 to 4).

Chapter 5 provides sample examination questions and model answers for both specifications.

Features of the new edition:

- The book has been re-designed so that topics are easily found.
- There are new topics such as team building, first aid, healthy eating, cooking methods, portion control and costing.
- Previously presented information, for example, environmental considerations and packaging, has been reviewed and up-dated.
- There are new sections on assessment criteria for both catering and hospitality, which have been written to help students complete controlled assessments.
- Much of the information is presented in chart or list form to try and minimise the amount of written text.
- The book provides students with information for independent study and revision.

- Activities are provided to help students check and improve their knowledge and understanding. They may be individual, group or whole class activities.
- Key words, terms and facts have been highlighted for quick reference and to focus learning.
- There is a glossary of terms and a comprehensive index for easy reference.
- 'Remember' boxes have been included to summarise important information.
- There are sample GCSE questions and answers so that students can develop their examination technique, review their performance and aid revision.

About the authors

Judy Gardiner is Principal Examiner for GCSE Catering for a major awarding body and an education consultant with many years of experience teaching Catering and Hospitality courses and training teachers.

Jacqui Housley is a Principal Examiner for GCSE Hospitality for a major awarding body and Head of Food at North Doncaster Technology College where she delivers GCSE courses in Hospitality and Catering and the Hospitality Diploma. She has over 20 years' experience working in the hospitality and catering industry.

Acknowledgements

The authors would like to thank their respective families for their continued support. They would also like to thank teachers for their generous comments and for contributing to the success of the previous edition of this book.

The authors and publishers would particularly like to extend their thanks and gratitude to Brigid O'Regan and Kay Walters, whose contributions and attention to detail have been invaluable.

Every effort has been made to trace the copyright holders of material reproduced here. The authors and publishers would like to thank the following for permission to reproduce copyright illustrations:

P.1 (top) © Nicola Gavin – Fotolia.com, (bottom) Photodisc/Getty Images; p.3 © Stephen McWilliam – Fotolia.com; p.4 (top) Photodisc/Getty Images, (bottom) Jeff Greenberg/Alamy; © Douglas Dean – Fotolia.com; p.6 (top) © Paco Ayala – Fotolia.com, (bottom) © Bill Grove/ iStockphoto.com; p.7 Anthony Blake/Fresh Food Images/Photolibrary.com; p.8 (top) © Nikolay Suslov - Fotolia.com, (bottom) © Michelangelo Gratton - Fotolia.com; p.9 Photodisc/Getty Images; p.13 Sam Bailey/Hodder Education; p.14 SCIMAT / SCIENCE PHOTO LIBRARY; p.16 (top) © Andrejs Pidjass - Fotolia.com, (bottom) Sam Bailey/Hodder Education; p.17 © Electronic Temperature Instruments Ltd; p.20 (bottom) Barking Dog Art; p.26 © Thomas Perkins/ iStockphoto.com; p.27 JANE SHEMILT/SCIENCE PHOTO LIBRARY; p.36 Sam Bailey/Hodder Education; p.37 (top) Sam Bailey/Hodder Education, (bottom) © John Panella - Fotolia.com; p.38 © Monika Adamczyk - Fotolia.com; p.39 (top) Sam Bailey/Hodder Education, (bottom) © Ingram Publishing Limited; pp.40-1 Sam Bailey/Hodder Education; p.42 (top) © Ingram Publishing Limited, (bottom) D. Hurst/Alamy; p.43 ALEAIMAGE/ iStockphoto.com; p.44 (top) © MARIA TOUTOUDAKI/ iStockphoto.com, (bottom) © Ingram Publishing Limited; p.45 (top) Sam Bailey/Hodder Education, (bottom) © Linda Hewell - Fotolia.com; pp.46-7 Sam Bailey/Hodder Education; p.48 (top) © Ingram Publishing Limited, (bottom) © Susanne Güttler - Fotolia.com; p.49 © Ingram Publishing Limited; p.50 Sam Bailey/Hodder Education; p.51 Sarah Bailey/Hodder Education; p.52 (top) © Joe Gough - Fotolia.com, (bottom) Sam Bailey/Hodder Education; p.53 Sam Bailey/Hodder Education; p.57 Sarah Bailey/Hodder Education; p.58 (top) © Ciaran Walsh/ iStockphoto.com, (2nd) Sarah Bailey/Hodder Education, (3rd) © Peter Galbraith/ iStockphoto.com, (bottom) © Rey Rojo/ iStockphoto.com; p. 59 (top) © Ryman Cabannes/photocuisine/Corbis, (others) Sarah Bailey/Hodder Education; p.60 Sarah Bailey/Hodder Education; p.61 © Andy Green - AGMIT/ iStockphoto.com; p.62 © iStockphoto.com; p.63 (top) ©Robert Linton/ iStockphoto.com, (bottom) © iStockphoto.com; p.66 Dominic Dibbs/Fresh Food Images/Photolibrary.com; pp.69-71 Barking Dog Art; p.74 (top) © Dinamir Predov/ iStockphoto.com, (bottom) Barking Dog Art; p.75 (top) © Olivier Blondeau/ iStockphoto.com, (bottom) wando studios inc/ iStockphoto.com; p.76 (top) ©2008 Colin & Linda McKie/ iStockphoto.com, (bottom) © iStockphoto.com; p.77 Crown copyright; p.78 D. Hurst/Alamy; p.79 (top) Sam Bailey/Hodder Education, (bottom) © Ingram Publishing Limited; p.80 Photodisc/Getty Images; p.82 Janet Kimber/The Image Bank/Getty Images; p.83 Lori Carpenter/age fotostock/Photolibrary.com; pp.84–5 Photodisc/Getty Images; p.86 Sam Bailey/Hodder Education; p.87 © Peter Spiro - Fotolia.com; p.88 © Norman Pogson - Fotolia.com; p. 89 (top) © Olaf Doering / Alamy, (2nd) Sam Bailey/Hodder Education, (bottom) © Sylvie Peruzzi - Fotolia.com; p.91 © Ingram Publishing Limited; p.92 © Lightworks Media / Alamy; p.95 © Marcel Pelletier/ iStockphoto.com; p.97 © Emrah Turudu/ iStockphoto.com; p.98 © Eric Tadsen/ iStockphoto.com; p.99 Webstream / Alamy; p.100 © Lucky Dragon - Fotolia.com; p.101 © Francois E. du Plessis - Fotolia.com; p.102 (top) © Marti

Acknowledgements

Timple - Fotolia.com, (bottom) Photodisc/Getty Images; p.108 (top) © 2007 David Franklin/ iStockphoto.com, (2nd) © Stockbyte/Getty Images, (3rd) © malcolm romain/ iStockphoto.com, (bottom) © Ingram Publishing Limited; p.110 (top) © René Mansi/ iStockphoto.com, (bottom) © Ingram Publishing Limited; p.116 © Elke Dennis - Fotolia.com; p.120 © Nataliya Kuznetsova - Fotolia.com; p.121 © Lori Sparkia – Fotolia.com; p.124 ©Damir Cudic/ iStockphoto.com; p.126 © Michael Chamberlin – Fotolia; p.128 (top) © Mikhail Zakharov/ iStockphoto.com, (bottom) © Valerie Loiseleux/ iStockphoto.com; p.130 (top) © Steven Allan/ iStockphoto.com, (bottom) © iStockphoto.com; p.131 © Serghei Starus/ iStockphoto.com; p.132 © Roy Shakespeare - Fotolia.com; p.133 (top) © Nikolay Suslov - Fotolia.com, (bottom) © Roman Milert - Fotolia.com; p.134 © Chantal SEIGNEURGENS - Fotolia.com; p.135 © SERDAR YAGCI/ iStockphoto.com; p.137 (top) © Eric Lecas - Fotolia.com, (bottom) © Robert Byron - Fotolia.com; p.138 © Richard Johnson - Fotolia.com; p.139 (top) Sam Bailey/Hodder Education, (bottom) © Ingram Publishing Limited; p.141 (top left) A. T. Willett / Alamy, (top right) Sam Bailey/Hodder Education, (middle) Carl Drury/Hodder Education, (bottom) © Scott Rothstein/ iStockphoto.com; p.143 (top) © Jeff Greenberg / Alamy, (bottom) © Edyta Pawlowska - Fotolia.com; p.144 (top) © Ingram Publishing Limited, (bottom) © Petr Vaclavek - Fotolia.com; p.146 (top) © Leah-Anne Thompson - Fotolia.com, (2nd) Carl Drury/Hodder Education, (3rd) © Elena Kalistratova - Fotolia.com, (bottom) Photodisc/Getty Images; p.147 Sam Bailey/Hodder Education; p.148 © Damir Cudic/ iStockphoto.com; p.150 (top) © Alfonso d'Agostino - Fotolia.com, (bottom) Photodisc/Getty Images; p.154 © Vasko Miokovic/ iStockphoto.com; p.156 © Troy McCullough - Fotolia.com; p.160 (top) Visit Wales, (bottom) © Vitalina Rybakova/ iStockphoto.com; p.162 © Rob Wilkinson / Alamy; p.163 (top) © Mark Stokes/ iStockphoto.com, (bottom) © Kevin Penhallow - Fotolia.com; p.164 (top) © Jan Kranendonk - Fotolia.com, (bottom) © Stef Feijen - Fotolia.com; p.167 (top) © Jan Kranendonk/ iStockphoto.com, (middle) © SELCUK ARSLAN - Fotolia.com, (bottom) © Andrea Seemann - Fotolia.com; p.168 © Roman Mostakov - Fotolia.com; p.169 © Nicola Di Nozzi - Fotolia.com; p.170 © Jacob Wackerhausen - Fotolia.com; p.172 © Dmitry Goygel-Sokol - Fotolia.com; p.178 (top) © Tomasz Stelmach - Fotolia.com, (bottom) Jim Green/fStop/Getty Images; p.180 (bottom) © Ingram Publishing Limited; p.181 © Olivier Blondeau/ iStockphoto.com; p.186 © iStockphoto.com; pp.190–9 © Ingram Publishing Limited.

Crown copyright material is reproduced with the permission of the Controller of HMSO and the Queen's Printer for Scotland

CHAPTER 1

GCSE CATERING (SINGLE AWARD)

1.1 THE INDUSTRY: FOOD AND DRINK

The catering industry is very diverse. A catering establishment is defined as one that provides food and/or drink. This is known as a product-and-service provider.

Many different kinds of commercial (for money) businesses operate in the catering industry, but there are also non-commercial businesses in the industry.

Types of establishment

Residential establishments that provide food and/or drink include:

- hotels
- guest houses
- holiday parks
- farmhouses
- public houses
- bed-and-breakfasts.

Non-residential establishments that provide food and/or drink. These include:

- restaurants
- cafes
- fast-food outlets
- public houses
- wine bars
- delicatessen and salad bars
- take-away outlets
- school meals and transport catering
- burger vans.

There are also **non-commercial residential establishments** within the industry. These include:

- hospitals
- residential homes
- prisons
- armed services.

Contract caterers

There are also caterers who provide food and drink for a function where catering facilities are not already provided. These are known as contract caterers.

They prepare the food for functions such as weddings, banquets, garden parties and parties in private houses. They may prepare and cook the food in advance and deliver it to the venue, or they may cook it on site. They may also provide staff to serve the food, if required. Contract caterers are used by a wide range of organisations as it relieves them of the pressures involved in catering for such events.

A range of food service systems are available. These include:

- counter service – cafeteria service, multi-point, free-flow, fast-food, vended service, seated counter service, buffet and carvery
- table service – waiter or waitress service
- transported meal systems – e.g. meals on aeroplanes
- cooking and/or service of food from a trolley in front of customers – e.g. Gueridon service.

Sometimes, more than one type of service operates within the same establishment. A central production area may send food to a variety of different outlets within one area.

Types of counter service

Cafeteria service

This is the most versatile of all food service systems. A menu is displayed at the entrance to the cafeteria.

- Customers 'flow' past a display of food and select the items they want. Some of the meal items (usually hot items such as main courses) may be served by staff from behind the counter.
- Payment is made before the customer eats. It is easy for staff to display the menu and stock the displays.
- Cutlery and condiments are placed after the tills to keep a steady flow.
- The dining area is regularly cleaned.
- Some areas of the dining room may be kept for customers eating meals rather than snacks at busy times.

Free-flow

This is similar to the cafeteria system, except that customers go straight to the food or drink counter they want. It avoids unnecessary queuing but is not good for people who want a full range of items.

Multi-point

This is like the free-flow system, but has separate trays, tills, cutlery and condiment areas. It's not good for customers who want a full range of items.

Fast-food

In fast-food outlets, the customer orders and collects the meal from one of a number of service points along the service counter.

- At each service point there is a cash till and a member of staff who takes the order, receives the payment, collects the food and drinks ordered and assembles them on a tray, to be eaten in the restaurant or in a bag or container to be taken away.
- The food is usually shown in photographs above the counter. The complex tills record all the orders, time, method of payment etc. and give a complete breakdown of sales and other information to head office. Speed is essential.
- Fast-food outlets are very expensive to set up and need expensive equipment (fryers, griddles, etc.). A fast-food outlet will not survive unless it has a high turnover of customers.

Many take-away restaurants, such as fish and chip shops and Chinese take-aways, use a similar method but only have one service point behind the counter.

ACTIVITY

Find out about the types of service offered in food outlets in your area. How many different ones can you find?

Vended service

This is used widely in large buildings, such as hospitals, hotels and factories, where food and drinks are needed throughout the day and night.

- Vending machines 'sell' a wide range of products such as sweets, drinks, packaged snacks and even whole plated meals.

- Some are 'coin operated' some are operated by special discs or cards issued to staff, some are 'free vend', i.e. operated by the touch of a button.
- Vending machines offer ideal portion control and good hygiene standards (food is always packaged).
- They need careful maintenance and regular stocking.
- High turnover is important. Vending machines are often placed next to microwaves so that customers can buy 'chilled' food and re-heat before eating, i.e. Buy – Reheat – Serve – Eat.

Seated counter service

Customers are seated at the counter, usually on stools, and are served by staff behind the counter. Often used in situations where customers are on their own (e.g. railway stations and airport terminals).

Buffet service

Customers select their meal items from an open counter or buffet table. The customers help themselves to everything, or the serving staff serve some or all of the items. Serving staff often serve the meat items as these are the most expensive, leaving customers to help themselves to salads, etc.

Carvery service

In this case, starters, drinks and sweets are served by the serving staff.

- Customers collect their own main course items from the carving table where the joints of meat are displayed and kept hot by special lamps and hot plates.
- Often, a chef from the kitchen carves the joints, but sometimes a member of the serving staff does the carving.
- Customers help themselves to vegetables, gravy, sauces and other accompaniments like Yorkshire puddings.
- Carveries are particularly popular for Sunday lunch.

Table service

Waiter/waitress service

This is used when a more personal service is needed.

- It is more expensive than a counter service, because of the number of staff involved.
- For large functions (e.g. wedding receptions and banquets) a waiter/waitress can serve many more people than in the usual restaurant service.
- When tables are laid up banquet style, one waiter/waitress would serve the people on both sides of an 'aisle', i.e. serve the left-hand side of one table and the right-hand side of the other table.

Transported meal systems

The most well known type of transported meals is airline food. This is used most commonly on long-haul flights, where passengers choose hot food from a limited menu.

How the airline food system works:

1. Airline representatives choose from a selection of prepared foods.
2. Food is prepared in the kitchens away from the airport.
3. Meals for special diets are ordered and prepared in the correct quantities by the kitchen.
4. Meals are plated, covered and blast chilled.
5. Meals are placed on trolleys covered with dry ice pellets to keep the food fresh.
6. The trolleys are delivered to the correct flights and stored in the kitchen area of the plane.
7. Before service the meals are re-heated and placed in heated trolleys.
8. Passengers then get a limited choice of meals on the plane.

Advantages:

- Children and special diets are catered for.
- The airline orders the right amount of dishes so there is less waste.
- First- and business-class passengers can pre-order their meals in advance.

Disadvantages:

- There are no 'second helpings'.
- The choice is limited to two dishes.
- Passengers do not always like the choices available.

The Gueridon system

This style of service is used with à la carte or table d'hôte menus. The food is carved or 'finished' at a table or trolley placed next to the customer's table. A spirit lamp is used to finish cooking portions of poultry, meat or fish. Some dishes are completed in this way, with a flambé technique or sauce. Two popular dishes are Steak Diane and Crèpes Suzette. This form of service requires highly skilled staff who can cook and present the food attractively and can work confidently with a little bit of 'showmanship'.

Job roles

There is a range of jobs available in the catering industry.

They can be split into three main groups:

- management and administration
- food preparation
- food and drink service.

Within each of these groups there are various jobs. Let's look briefly at each area.

Management

There may be a manager for all the different areas of a large establishment, but only one in a smaller place. Within a larger company there may be:

- a manager, who is in charge of the day-to-day running of the company, and is responsible for making a profit and organising every area.
- an assistant manager, who is responsible to the manager and may have work delegated to him/her by the manager. He/she will also be in charge in the manager's absence.

Chefs

Depending on the size of the establishment, there may only be one chef with a kitchen porter to help, or there may be a whole brigade of chefs. A 'brigade' is the term used for a group of chefs in a kitchen. There are several different kinds:

- The head chef is the person in charge of the kitchen. In a large establishment, this person has the title of 'executive chef'. The executive chef is a manager who is responsible for all aspects of food production, including menu planning, purchasing, costing, planning work schedules, and hygiene.
- The second (sous) chef ('soo shef') is directly in charge of production. Because the executive chef's responsibilities require spending a great deal of time in the office, the sous chef takes command of the actual production and the minute-by-minute supervision of the staff. Both the

sous chef and executive chef have had many years of experience in all stations of the kitchen.

- The pastry chef (patissier) ('pa-tees-syay') prepares pastries and desserts.
- The larder chef (garde manger) ('gard-mawn-zhay') is responsible for cold foods, including salads and dressings, patés, cold hors d'oeuvres, and buffet items.
- The sauce chef (saucier) ('so-see-ay') prepares sauces, stews, and hot hors d'oeuvres, and sautés foods to order. This is usually the highest position of all the stations.
- The vegetable chef (entremetier) (awn-truh-met-i-ay) prepares vegetables, soups, starches and eggs. Large kitchens may divide these duties among the vegetable cook, the fry cook and the soup cook.
- The assistant chef (commis) helps in all areas of the kitchen, generally doing the easier tasks. The commis may be completing basic training to become a chef.
- The kitchen porters clean up after the chefs, do the washing and carry goods to and from the store.

Food and drink service

This section covers the staff who serve food and drink to the customers. These staff are collectively known as 'waiting staff'. They may include:

- the restaurant manager, who is in charge of the restaurant. The manager takes bookings, relays information to the head chef, arranges training for staff, completes rotas and ensures the restaurant runs smoothly.
- the head waiter/ess, who is second in charge of the restaurant. They greet and seat customers and relay information to the staff. They may also deal with complaints.
- the wine waiter/ess, who is responsible for helping guests to select wine. They serve the wine and other alcoholic drinks to customers.
- the waiting staff, who serve the customers, clear the tables and check that the customers are satisfied with the service.

ACTIVITY

Choose a local establishment and find out whether or not they employ local staff and use local produce and services. Make a list or table to show your findings.

Employment providers

Establishments within the hospitality and catering sectors all provide employment for the community they are in. The company may also buy local produce for the meals and services they provide. We are being encouraged to cut down our carbon footprint and the amount of miles that food goods travel, so it is beneficial to the local community if the establishment buys local produce and uses local services such as electricians, florists and plumbers. Hospitality establishments may include information about locally grown or reared produce that feature on their menus to encourage customers to buy them.

Employment opportunities

Workers employed by the companies could be full-time, part-time or casual staff.

- Full-time staff have permanent jobs in the establishment and work all year. They should have a contract with their terms of employment set out in writing. They could work set shifts or shifts that change daily depending on how busy the establishment is. They will often work a set amount of days over a seven-day week, including weekends.
- Part-time staff may work on set days of the week, or have set shifts. They may be employed permanently, but do fewer hours a week than full-time staff, often working during the busier times of the day such as service of meals.
- Casual staff work for specific functions and are often employed through an agency. They do not have a contract or set hours to work, but are called in during busier times of the year, such as Christmas. Often, casual staff work for the same establishment each year as they know their way round and know how the company works. However, this is not always the case and some casual staff do not know where they will be working until the week before.

Career paths

There are many career paths within the industry and a range of jobs can be found in the different sectors. For example, a person could be employed in the kitchen of a restaurant and then move to a hotel and progress from there into management.

Most people who go into the hospitality and catering industry are able to work their way up to the position they would like. It is a great industry to be involved in and you can often meet famous people on the way. Larger establishments offer the opportunity to work in a range of areas and provide training on the job. The advantage of this is you can earn at the same time. You can also go on day release or attend college full time.

Working in the catering industry gives you the opportunity to travel if you wish to. Jobs are available locally, nationally and internationally. Jobs are often advertised in local newspapers and in catering magazines such as *The Caterer*, as well as on the internet. It is very easy to find out the jobs that are available through job centres, the press and websites. Many larger companies   and chains advertise jobs on their websites. They are often updated regularly so it is worth checking daily. Also, your local college will have links with various hotels and restaurants and are a good source of knowledge when it comes to applying for jobs.

Assistant chef, Anglia Hotel

Cambridge
Full-time
Competitive salary

In this role you will assist the kitchen staff with the day-to-day running of the kitchen, and prepare food to a high standard. At the Anglia Hotel Restaurant, we offer an à la carte menu with daily specials to showcase the best local, organic food.

We are looking for someone who is passionate about food and about hospitality. Previous experience is not essential, but commitment and enthusiasm are.

We offer an excellent package of benefits, and you will receive a share of the service charge earned. We also run a training and development programme and encourage all staff to work towards further qualifications. The Anglia Hotel offers many opportunities for a rewarding career.

TERMINOLOGY:

Management: the people who are in charge of specific areas.

Chefs: the staff who are responsible for preparing and cooking the food.

Food and drink service: the serving area in a restaurant, café, bar.

ACTIVITY

Find out what jobs are available in your area. Research how you can progress up the ladder and what qualifications you would need to be able to do the job.

With the help of your teacher, carry out a mock interview for a job you would like to do.

List the personal skills you would need to work in the hospitality and catering industry.

HEALTH, SAFETY AND HYGIENE

Food poisoning

What is food poisoning?

Food poisoning is an illness you get by eating contaminated food. Food is contaminated if there is something in it which should not be there, things like bacteria and other microbes (viruses, moulds).

Other causes of food poisoning include:

● eating food that contains chemicals and metals.
● eating poisonous plants (e.g. toadstools, berries).

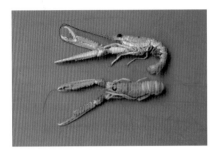

Shellfish

High-risk foods

Bacteria really like foods that are moist and high in protein. These include:

● meat
● poultry
● eggs
● stocks
● shellfish
● cooked rice.

● fish
● dairy products
● gravies
● sauces
● seafood

Cooked rice

Why bacteria make us ill

Some bacteria have to be inside your body to make you ill. Once inside you, the bacteria attack your body causing illness. Some produce a toxin (poison) on the food which makes you ill when you eat it.

How bacteria multiply

Bacteria reproduce rapidly by dividing into two, which is known as binary fission.

Each bacterium only needs 10–20 minutes to multiply.

● 1 bacterium = millions in a few hours.
● ideal conditions for growth: food + moisture + warmth + time.

> ### Symptoms of food poisoning
>
> Abdominal pain – pain in the abdomen (stomach-ache)
> Diarrhoea – 'the runs'
> Vomiting – being sick
> Nausea – the feeling of sickness
> Fever – a raised temperature
>
> Symptoms vary depending on the type of food poisoning and can last for days.

Critical temperatures

High-risk and perishable foods should be kept out of the danger zone temperatures of between 5°C and 63°C.

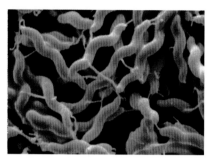

Campylobacter

> **!P REMEMBER**
>
> Remember, bacteria need four things to multiply: food, warmth, time and moisture.

Types of food poisoning bacteria	

Campylobacter	• Found in raw poultry and meat.
	• Illness caused by small numbers of bacteria.
	• Symptoms:
	  – fever
	  – headache
	  – abdominal pain
	  – diarrhoea
	  – can last for 10 days.

Salmonella	• Found in raw meat, unwashed vegetables, poultry and eggs.
	• Second most common cause of food poisoning.
	• Survives refrigeration.
	• Illness caused by large numbers of bacteria.
	• Symptoms:
	  – fever
	  – can be fatal!
	  – diarrhoea
	  – vomiting
	  – abdominal pain
	  – can take up to 48 hours for symptoms to show
	  – can last for 3 weeks.

Types of food poisoning bacteria

E Coli 0157	• Found in the gut of animals and humans.
	• E Coli 0157 is found in raw and undercooked meats, raw vegetables.
	• Illness caused by small numbers of bacteria.
	• Can survive refrigeration and freezing.
	• Symptoms:
	  – diarrhoea
	  – can be fatal
	  – can take up to 5 days for symptoms to show.

Clostridium Perfringens	• From animal faeces.
	• Found in soil, manure, sewage, raw meat and poultry.
	• Produces spores which may not be killed by cooking.
	• Symptoms:
	  – abdominal pain
	  – diarrhoea
	  – nausea
	  – can be fatal
	  – onset normally after 8–18 hours.

Listeria	• Found in soil, vegetation, meat, poultry, soft cheese, salad vegetables.
	• Can grow at low temperatures.
	• Symptoms:
	  – range from flu-like symptoms to meningitis
	  – pregnant women, the very old and the very young are most at risk
	  – can take up to weeks to develop.

Bacillus Cereus	• Found in soil and dust.
	• Frequently in rice dishes and sometime in pasta, meat or vegetable dishes.
	• Illness can be caused by a small number of bacteria.
	• Forms spores that are resistant to heat.
	• Symptoms (two types of illness):
	  – diarrhoea, abdominal pain after 8–18 hours
	  – vomiting after 1–5 hours
	  – usually lasts less than 24 hours.

Staphylococcus Aureus	• Found on the skin, in cuts and boils and up the nose.
	• Transferred to food from hands, nose or mouth.
	• Large numbers needed to cause illness.
	• Survives refrigeration.
	• Produces a toxin which may survive cooking.
	• Symptoms:
	  – severe vomiting
	  – abdominal pains
	  – diarrhoea
	  – onset within 6 hours
	  – lasts about 2 days.

The 1995 Food Safety (General Food Hygiene) Regulations

Why do we have food hygiene regulations?

We have food hygiene regulations to prevent outbreaks of food poisoning.

Customers need to know that food is safe to eat. Food safety regulations are constantly changing and establishments should follow the latest guidelines. For example in 2006, regulations were updated and 'Safer Food Better Business' was introduced. Food safety and hygiene regulations are enforced by EHOs (Environmental Health Officers) who regularly check all food premises.

What are the main requirements of the regulations?

The food hygiene regulations cover three main areas:

- food premises
- personal hygiene of employees
- hygienic practices.

Food premises

Food premises must:

- be well maintained
- be regularly cleaned
- have lockers for employees
- have hand-wash facilities provided
- have clean cloakroom and toilet facilities
- have first aid available
- have clean storage areas
- have temperature-controlled fridges and freezers
- have equipment that is clean and in good working order
- be free from pets, pests, etc.

Personal hygiene of food handlers

Food handlers should:

- have regular training in food safety
- be dressed in clean 'whites' or other uniform
- have hair tied back (and ideally wear a hat)

- have short, clean nails – no nail varnish or jewellery
- be in good health (they cannot work with upset stomachs)
- have 'good' habits, e.g. no coughing or sneezing over food
- wash their hands after handling raw meat, after blowing nose, after going to the toilet, etc.

Cuts should be covered with coloured waterproof plasters.

Hygienic practices

- Food deliveries should be checked thoroughly.
- Food should be labelled and stored correctly (in freezers, chillers, fridges and dry stores).
- Food should be 'rotated' (first in, first out).
- Care should be taken with temperature control in the kitchen (i.e. food kept out of the danger zone of 5°–63°C).
- Food should be prepared quickly and as close to cooking time as possible.
- Hot food should be maintained at above 63°C.
- The core temperature of cooked food needs to be at least 75°C.
- Chilled food should be stored below 5°C.
- Washing up should be done in hot soapy water if there is no dishwasher available.
- Waste should be disposed of safely.

Now wash your hands please

ACTIVITY

Give five reasons why safer food leads to better business.

Find out what qualifications are available in food safety and hygiene.

Find out about the role of the EHO.

A temperature probe

Food handling

High standards of personal, food and kitchen hygiene are needed to keep food safe and prevent food poisoning.

What do we mean by personal hygiene?

Good personal hygiene means ensuring that germs found in or on the body do not transfer to food. We need to have high standards of personal hygiene or cleanliness.

TERMINOLOGY:

EHO: Environmental Health Officer

Regulations: Legal requirements

Core temperature: The temperature in the middle of the food

Personal appearance of kitchen staff

Long hair tied back

Discreet make-up

Neckerchief to absorb
sweat from neck

Nails short and clean
No nail varnish

No jewellery (except wedding ring)

No heavy perfume, scent or
aftershave

Cuts covered with
blue waterproof plasters

Loose-fitting trousers

Flat, comfortable shoes non-slip
with protective toe caps for kitchen

No facial piercing

Wearing of hat

Clear complexion

Daily shower or bath

No body odour (B.O.)

Correct clean uniform

No illness or stomach
complaints

All food handlers should:

- wash hands before handling food
- wash hands when changing from one food to another
- wash hands after going to the toilet, blowing nose,
  smoking or handling waste
- have short clean nails
- cover cuts and sores with blue waterproof detectable
  plasters
- be in good health
- tie back long hair, or preferably cover it with a hat
- be dressed appropriately in clean clothes – 'whites'
- taste food with a clean teaspoon which is then washed.

All food handlers should *not*:

- wear outdoor coats in the kitchen
- wear nail varnish, false nails or jewellery
- work when suffering from stomach upsets, sickness or
  diarrhoea
- smoke, eat or drink around the food
- cough or sneeze over food.

What do we mean by food hygiene?

Good food hygiene means ensuring food is safe to eat so that it does not give customers food poisoning.

Food handlers should:

- store foods at the correct temperature (chilled food under 5°C, frozen food under −18°C)
- defrost frozen foods thoroughly before cooking
- keep food cool, clean and covered
- prepare food as close to cooking or serving time as possible
- take steps to prevent cross-contamination
- use colour-coded boards and knives
- separate raw and cooked foods
- prepare food on clean work surfaces
- sanitise work surfaces and equipment regularly
- adopt a 'clean-as-you-go' routine
- cook foods at a high enough temperature for a long enough time to kill bacteria
- use a temperature probe to check core temperature of food
- wash fruit and vegetables before use
- check 'use by' and 'best before' dates
- use pasteurised egg products, if appropriate, for 'high risk' dishes
- clean all equipment used in preparation of food thoroughly
- dispose of waste hygienically
- cool or chill food rapidly so that it is out of the danger zone (5°C to 63°C) where bacteria multiply rapidly
- re-heat food thoroughly (but do not serve to 'high risk' groups)
- refrigerate and cover food trolleys and buffets
- check fridge temperature at least three times a day.

Food handlers should *not*:

- top up 'high risk' foods like mayonnaise on salad bars
- reheat food for 'high-risk' groups.

> **Colour codes**
>
> Red: raw meat
> Blue: raw fish
> Yellow: cooked fish
> Green: salad and fruit
> Brown: vegetables
> White: bakery and dairy

What do we mean by kitchen hygiene?

Good kitchen hygiene means ensuring kitchens are clean and well organised so that customers are not at risk of food poisoning.

Kitchens should:

- have a cleaning schedule

> **Example of a cleaning schedule**
>
> What is to be cleaned?
> Who will carry out the cleaning?
> When the cleaning needs to be done (e.g. daily, weekly, monthly).
> How the cleaning is to be done (e.g. methods and standards).
> The time needed for the cleaning.
> The cleaning materials to be used (chemicals, materials and equipment).
> Safety precautions (e.g. wearing of gloves, goggles, etc).
> Signature of person carrying out the cleaning, and signature of supervisor.

- have good ventilation, lighting and extraction fans if needed
- have clean well-ventilated food stores
- rotate stock so that the oldest stock is used first (damaged canned or packaged food should not be used)
- have freezers and fridges with visible temperature controls
- clean and check freezers and fridges regularly (out-of-date food should be thrown out)
- wash dirty pans, cutlery and crockery as soon as possible
- have designated hand-wash and cloakroom areas
- have floors, walls and work surfaces that are easy to clean and sanitise
- mop up spillages immediately
- wipe down surfaces regularly (do not allow food crumbs to accumulate)
- have high standards of waste disposal
- ensure that all bins are covered with lids so that vermin/pests cannot gain access
- have good pest control, i.e. insect-o-cutors, window mesh etc.
- report cases of infestation of insects (flies, cockroaches) or rodents (rats and mice) immediately.

Damage caused by flies and rats

> **ACTIVITY**
>
> Look at the picture on the next page. If you were appointed as Head Chef, what would you need to do to ensure higher standards of food safety?

Accident prevention

A catering kitchen can be a dangerous place. Here are the main dangers and ways of preventing accidents in the kitchen.

Floors

Mop up spills immediately.

Keep floors clean and grease-free.

Do not leave equipment in 'pathways' used in the kitchen.

Repair damaged floor surfaces quickly.

Knives

Use the right-sized knife for the food you are cutting.

Keep handles clean and grease-free.

Keep knives sharp – blunt knives need too much pressure.

Do not leave knives on edges of chopping boards or tables.

Do not put knives in washing-up bowls or point up in a dishwasher.

Do not try to catch a falling knife.

Electrical equipment

Check machinery is in good working order.

Check electrical wires are not frayed or worn.

Do not handle electrical equipment with wet hands.

Check safety notices.

Assemble equipment correctly and use safety guards.

> **!P REMEMBER**
>
> Some machinery (electrical equipment) cannot be operated by people who are under 18.

Saucepans

Indicate hot handles by sprinkling flour on them.

Take care when moving or lifting heavy pans.

Use oven gloves or oven cloths.

Turn pan handles towards the back of the cooker.

Do not use wet cloths for hot pans.

Fryers

Do not fill above the fat level indicated (usually up to half full).

Do not put wet foods into fryers.

Lower food into fryer carefully.

Change fat regularly.

Foods

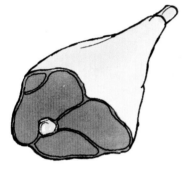

Be aware that fish bones and meat bones can cause cuts.

Be aware that frozen food can cause 'burns'.

Take care when opening and disposing of cans and jars.

Store raw and cooked foods separately.

Storing equipment

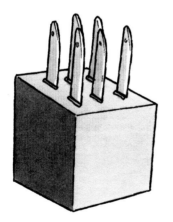

Store all equipment safely, e.g. knives in a knife block.

Unplug electrical equipment when not in use.

Replace safety guards on electrical equipment.

Fires

Do not have flames larger than the size of the pan.

Do not leave cloths or oven gloves over cookers.

Time the cooking of foods accurately.

Take special care when cooking in fat – it can spit and set alight.

Have fire blankets and fire extinguishers to hand.

Have clear fire procedures.

Clothing

Wear appropriate clothing in the kitchen.

Wear non-slip shoes or clogs.

Do not wear jewellery that can become trapped in machinery.

Tie long hair back. Cover hair with a hat.

Behaviour

Do not run in the kitchen.

Pay attention when given instructions or orders.

Concentrate on the job 'in hand'.

Make sure that workers are supervised at all times.

Cleaning

Try to 'clean as you go'.

Keep cleaning materials and equipment away from food areas.

Use the right cleaning materials for the task.

Do not 'mix' cleaning materials.

Use cleaning materials at the right strength.

Store cleaning materials and equipment carefully.

Hazard Analysis Critical Control Points (HACCP)

Food hygiene laws mean that *all* businesses should have a Hazard Analysis Critical Control Points (HACCP) system in place.

Food producers need to understand *how*, *why* and *where* food could become contaminated and then set out to prevent it from happening. The HACCP system helps them to do this.

Food producers (this includes hotel and restaurant owners, not just food manufacturers) need to:

- have an HACCP system in place
- draw up a flow chart of **each step** in the preparation of **each dish** – starting with the buying of ingredients and ending with sale to the customer
- **analyse each step** of the process to see what could go wrong and could result in a danger to the customer (dangers or hazards include bacteria, chemicals and foreign bodies)
- identify what can be done to **control the hazards**, e.g. separate raw and cooked food to prevent cross-contamination, have high standards of personal hygiene to avoid contamination, use correct cooking times and temperatures to kill bacteria
- **set standards** (known as critical limits) for each control point. This will state the conditions that **must be met** to ensure food is safe to eat. These controls must be checked regularly. Records must be kept to show the controls are working
- **review HACCP** whenever there is a change to a recipe or a new dish on the menu or a change of activity in the kitchen. Otherwise, HACCP must be reviewed once a year
- keep all documentation and records safe.

Critical control points for catering

Step	Hazard	Action
1 Purchase	High-risk foods such as cooked meat could be contaminated with food-poisoning bacteria when you buy them.	– Buy from a supplier with a good reputation. – Specify a maximum temperature for food when it is delivered.
2 Receipt of food		– Check that food looks, smells and feels right when it is delivered. – Check the temperature of food.
3 Storage	Food-poisoning bacteria could grow on high-risk foods and contaminate other food.	– Keep high-risk food at a safe temperature and wrapped up. – Label food with a 'sell-by' date and use it up by that date. – Rotate stock so that the oldest food is used up before the 'sell-by' date.
4 Preparation	High-risk food could be contaminated with food-poisoning bacteria. Bacteria could grow.	– Wash your hands before you handle food. – Don't keep food out at room temperature more than you have to. – Use clean equipment. – Use different equipment for high-risk foods and other foods. – Separate raw foods from cooked foods.
5 Cooking	Food-poisoning bacteria could survive during cooking.	– Cook chicken, rolled joints and re-formed meat such as burgers so that the thickest part reaches 75°C. – Sear the outside of other meat (such as steaks) before cooking.
6 Cooling	Surviving food-poisoning bacteria could grow. Bacteria could produce poisons.	– Cool food as fast as possible. – Don't leave food to cool at room temperature unless it's only for a very short time. For example, put rice into a shallow dish so that it will cool quickly.
7 Hot-holding (keeping food hot, e.g. in a self-service cafeteria)		– Keep food at 63°C or hotter.
8 Reheating	Food-poisoning bacteria could survive during reheating.	– Reheat food to 75°C or higher.
9 Chilled storage	Food-poisoning bacteria could grow.	– Keep the storage temperature right. – Label high-risk foods with the correct 'sell-by' date.
10 Serving	Food-poisoning bacteria could grow, causing disease. Bacteria could produce poisons.	– Serve cold food as soon as possible after you remove it from the fridge, so that it doesn't get warm. – Serve hot food quickly so that it doesn't cool down.

Adapted from Department of Health guidelines

HACCP checklist for businesses

1. Provide food hygiene training.
2. Remind staff of the importance of personal hygiene.
3. Get staff to report illnesses.
4. Always monitor food safety controls (temperature of fridges etc).
5. Know your suppliers and check all supplies on delivery.
6. Separate raw and cooked food.
7. Have adequate washing facilities.
8. Take measures to avoid cross-contamination (i.e. put up hand-wash notices, colour-coded boards and knives, cleaning charts, good cleaning schedules).
9. Maintain food temperature controls (i.e. avoid danger zone of 5°C to 63°C, serve chilled food under 5°C and serve hot food above 63°C).
10. Have an effective cleaning programme.

First aid

A first aid box

Even in the most organised kitchens, accidents can happen, so it is important to know some basic first aid.

First aid is based on three principles, known as the three Ps. The three Ps are:

- to promote recovery
- to prevent further injury
- to protect the patient.

Note: A person who has no first aid training should not give an injured person medical treatment or anything to eat or drink but they can reassure the patient and keep them calm and comfortable until medical help arrives.

First aid legislation

- There must be at least one first aid box for every 150 people.
- There must be at least one named qualified first aider for every 150 people.
- There must be a 'responsible person' in charge of first aid.
- First aid boxes must be regularly checked for their content.
- First aid boxes must be easily accessible (easily available).

First aid boxes should contain the following:

- sterile dressings
- wound dressings
- adhesive (sticky) plaster
- sterile cotton wool/eye pad
- pressure bandages
- safety pins, scissors, eye bath and tweezers
- rubber/latex/plastic gloves
- triangular bandages.

Simple first aid

The most common accidents that happen in a catering kitchen are burns, scalds, cuts and falls.

Burns and scalds

A burn is caused by dry heat, e.g. from a hot pan or cooker. A scald is caused by moist heat, e.g. from steam or boiling water. Both can be extremely painful. To treat a burn or scald effectively you need to cool the area of skin that has been affected. Immediately place under cold running water and leave for at least 10 minutes or until the stinging sensation stops. Do not apply cream, as this will 'seal' the heat in. For burns or scalds larger than a 10p piece, get medical advice.

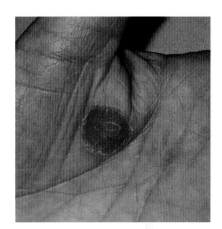

A burn

Note: Water boils at 100°C, so a burn or scald caused by a hot pan, boiling water or steam can be very painful. However, burns caused by hot fat (which is used in fryers at a temperature of 180°C or more) can be very dangerous. If burns are caused by hot fat, seek medical help straight away.

Cuts

Wash, dry and apply a blue, waterproof, detectable plaster. If bleeding does not stop, hold the injured part (usually a finger) above the level of the heart and squeeze tightly.

Why are blue detectable plasters used in the food industry?

The plasters are bright blue so that they 'show up' easily in food. They also have a thin metal strip in them. At the end of the manufacturing process, all foods pass through an x-ray machine – the plaster would sound a warning and the food would be rejected!

Falls

Falls often happen when people slip on wet, greasy or dirty floors. Sometimes, slipping can just make you feel foolish, rather than actually hurt. Falls can also happen when people faint. For faints, loosen tight clothing and put the patient's head down between their knees. If the patient is lying on the floor, do not help them up. Place them in the recovery position and allow them to sit up slowly as soon as they feel able to do so.

Food Safety Act (1990)

The Food Safety Act covers food safety from raw ingredients through to finished products. The law concentrates on making sure food is safe to eat and is of the quality and composition that customers expect. The Act gives Environmental Health Officers the power to:

- enter any food premises at any time
- inspect food
- take samples of food away for analysis
- confiscate any food they judge to be unfit
- issue 'improvement notices' to food businesses
- close premises down.

The Food Safety Act links closely with Hazard Analysis Critical Control Points (HACCP) and Food Hygiene Regulations. The Act emphasises the need for a high level of personal hygiene amongst staff, good hygiene habits of staff, avoiding cross contamination, safe storage of food, good cleaning schedules and strict temperature controls. Under the Act food handlers and manufacturers may be prosecuted if their food is found to be unsafe to eat.

HACCP

HACCP stands for Hazard Analysis Critical Control Points. It is now a legal requirement for all food businesses to carry out some form of hazard analysis to identify the most critical (dangerous in terms of bacteria) areas of their business and to make sure they are under control.

Hazards

A hazard is something that has the potential to cause harm. In the food industry, hazards include those shown in the table overleaf.

Physical and chemical damage can often be seen. Food contaminated with bacteria however can look, smell and taste perfectly normal.

Type of hazard	Example
Biological	Salmonella in chicken
Chemical	Contamination from cleaning materials, e.g. bleach
Physical	Damaged packaging, glass found in food

Critical control points

There are areas in the food business where control is *essential* to reduce the risk of food poisoning. If a caterer 'gets it wrong' they could be breaking the law, so it is important to ensure every step from the purchasing of food through its preparation and serving is controlled.

ACTIVITY

Choose a food (e.g. frozen chicken breasts). Fill in the chart below, stating what the hazards/dangers might be at every stage and stating what action you would take to ensure your customers do not suffer from salmonella food poisoning.

HACCP chart

Food	Hazard	Action
Buying		
Delivery		
Storage		
Preparation		
Cooking		
Cooling		

Food Safety (General Food Hygiene) Regulations (1995)

These regulations cover three main areas:

- food premises
- personal hygiene of staff
- hygienic practices.

Food Labelling Regulations (2006)

By law, the following information should be on a label:

- 'use by' or 'best before' date
- list of ingredients in weight order, with the heaviest first
- name of manufacturer
- address of manufacturer
- name of the food and a brief description of the food (if it is not obvious)
- weight (the 'e' symbol shows average weight of similar packets) barcode – shows where and when manufactured and price
- special claims about the food (suitable for vegetarians, low in fat)
- method of storage, making, cooking.

Food manufacturers often include nutritional information, but report on fat, carbohydrate (starch with sugars), fibre and total kcal (energy value) only. Often vitamins and minerals are not included. There is continuing debate about the best way of giving nutritional information on food.

| **Display until:** 22 April | |
| **Use by:** 25 April | |

(Keep refrigerated)

Nutrition information
Typical values per 100 g:

Energy	199 kJ, 47 kcal
Protein	0.4 g
Carbohydrates	11.8 g
of which sugars	10.1 g
Fat	0.2 g
of which saturates	less than 0.1 g
Fibre	1.8 g
Sodium	less than 0.1 g

Fair trading, trades description and trading standards

The 'Trades Description Act' makes it a criminal offence to 'falsely describe' goods or services. Care must be taken when:

- wording the menu (e.g. frozen foods cannot be called fresh)
- describing menu items to customers
- letting customers know about extra costs, e.g. service charges
- describing service conditions.

Health and Safety at Work Act (1974)

This covers all aspects of health and safety at work. All employers must provide safe working areas. All employees must take care of their own health and safety and not endanger others.

Legal obligation of employers:

- To take responsibility for the health and safety of employees
- To provide adequate working space
- To provide safe areas of work
- To provide supervision, instruction and training of staff
- Safety and maintenance of machinery and tools
- Good ventilation, lighting and temperature control
- Easy evacuation and good exit routes (in case of fire or emergency)
- A safety policy document
- Risk assessment.

Legal obligation of employees:

- To take reasonable care of their own health and safety
- To take reasonable care of other people's health and safety
- Not to misuse equipment, machinery or premises.

The Health and Safety Executive (HSE) exists to protect people's health and safety by ensuring that risks are properly controlled. They provide many free information guides and leaflets about health and safety. They also enforce the regulations associated with health and safety and can visit and inspect premises whenever they choose.

The Health and Safety Executive (HSE) five-point plan

Health and safety law states that organisations must:

- Provide a written health and safety policy (if they employ five or more people)
- Assess risks to employees, customers, partners and any other people who could be affected by their activities
- Arrange for the effective planning, organisation, control, monitoring and review of preventive and protective measures
- Ensure they have access to competent health and safety advice
- Consult employees about their risks at work and current preventive and protective measures.

Failure to meet these requirements could have serious consequences. Sanctions and punishments include fines and imprisonment.

ACTIVITY

Many employers offer an induction training programme to new employees. Devise your own induction programme to cover:

- Health and safety
- Food safety
- First aid

Safety signs

There are many safety signs used in the catering industry. The most common ones are these:

- Warning signs – these are triangular. They have a black symbol on a yellow background, e.g. caution, trip hazard.

- Mandatory (must do) signs – these are circular. They have a white symbol on a blue background. They show things that must be done, e.g. wash hands.

- Prohibition (do not do) signs – these are circular. They have a black symbol on a white background. The circle is outlined in red and there is a thick diagonal line across it denoting things that must not be done, e.g. no mobile phones, no smoking.

- Emergency signs – these are square or rectangular. They have a white symbol on a green background, e.g. emergency exit sign.

- Fire-fighting signs – these are square or rectangular. They have a white symbol on a red background, e.g. fire reel.

ACTIVITY

Next time you visit a catering outlet see how many of the different signs you can see

Key points:

Safety signs can be:
● Warning
● Mandatory (must do)
● Prohibition (do not do)
● Emergency
● Fire-fighting

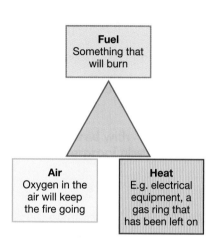

Fuel
Something that will burn

Air
Oxygen in the air will keep the fire going

Heat
E.g. electrical equipment, a gas ring that has been left on

Fire regulations

Fire prevention

Fires in catering establishments are fairly common and can result in injury or loss of life. A basic knowledge of fires should help in both preventing fires and extinguishing them quickly.

A fire needs three components:

● Fuel: something that burns
● Air: oxygen to keep fire going
● Heat: gas, electricity, etc.

To put out (extinguish) a fire the three main methods are

● Starving: removing the fuel
● Smothering: removing the air (oxygen)
● Cooling: removing the heat.

Fire alarms should be tested weekly and staff should be instructed in the use of fire-fighting equipment. Care must be taken to use the correct fire extinguisher, for example, water extinguishers should *not* be used on live electrical equipment because water is a conductor of electricity and the person holding the extinguisher could be electrocuted. Water extinguishers should also *not* be used in oil or fat fires because they cause ignited fat to spread and increase the heat. Although it may be possible to extinguish a small fire, never put yourself or others in danger.

Fire procedures

● Raise the alarm.
● Call the fire brigade.
● Turn off gas supply, electricity and fans if possible.
● Try to fight the fire with the appropriate extinguisher or fire blanket but do not put yourself in danger.
● Close doors and windows.
● Leave the building and go to the assembly point.

● **Do not** delay raising the alarm or calling the fire brigade.
● **Do not** use lifts.
● **Do not** stop to collect your belongings.

Fire safety regulations

New fire safety orders apply to the vast majority of premises and workplaces in the UK. The owners of premises (each owner is called a 'responsible person' in the orders) need to develop a fire policy that must:

- Reduce the risk of the outbreak of fire
- Reduce the risk of the spread of fire
- Provide means of escape
- Show preventative action.

The 'responsible person' needs to set up procedures for dealing with fires, which include:

- Having regular fire drills
- Identifying circumstances that trigger the emergency
- Identifying how evacuation should take place
- Identifying procedures for re-admitting people to premises
- Ensuring means of escape are available at all times
- Providing fire extinguishers
- Giving instruction to employees
- Ensuring people from outside the organisation are properly controlled and informed.

The 'responsible person' must carry out a fire risk assessment, which helps identify all the fire hazards and risks in the workplace. This risk assessment consists of five steps.

- Identifying the fire hazards
- Identifying people at risk
- Evaluating the risks
- Recording the findings
- Reviewing and revising the risk assessment.

The fire safety orders are enforced by the local Fire Brigade. However, there are other enforcing agencies such as the Health and Safety Executive (HSE), the Ministry of Defence (MOD) Fire Service and local authorities.

Throughout the course you will have plenty of opportunities to learn new practical skills. The following is a guide to the level of skill needed to prepare dishes. You should aim to develop for the higher-level skills and use them when you carry out practical work or take part in functions.

Skills and presentation

Fish is a high-risk food

Higher-level skills:

- Pastry making – short crust, pate sucre, choux.
- Roux-based sauces.
- Meringues and pavlovas.
- Meat and fish cookery (using high-risk foods).
- Decorated cakes and gateaux.
- Rich yeast doughs.
- Complex accompaniments and garnishes.

Medium-level skills:

- Basic bread doughs.
- Simple cakes, biscuits, cookies and scones.
- Vegetable and fruit dishes requiring even sizes, e.g. fruit salad, stir-fries that show competent knife skills.
- Cheesecakes and similar desserts.
- Simple sauces, e.g. red wine sauce.
- Puff pastry items that need shaping but use ready-made pastry.

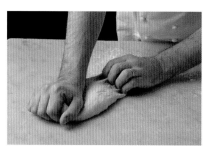

Kneading dough

Basic skills:

- Assembling products, e.g. using prepared sauces, bought meringue nests, etc.
- Crumbles.
- Sandwiches.
- Pizza with ready-made base.
- Jacket potatoes.
- Simple salads.

Presentation:

- The finished appearance overall – the 'look' of the dishes when presented.
- Colour.
- Use of decoration and garnish.
- Correct texture or consistency of food.
- Flavour and seasoning.
- Temperature of food (hot or cold as appropriate).
- Correct serving dishes.

Preparing different foods

Meat and poultry

In the UK we eat the meat of three main animals. These are pigs (ham, gammon, pork and bacon), sheep (lamb and mutton) and cows (beef and veal). We also eat poultry (chicken, turkey, goose and duck) and game birds such as partridge and pheasant. The edible internal organs of animals, known as offal (liver, kidneys, heart, etc.) are also eaten.

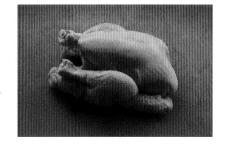

Most of the lamb we eat comes from animals that are less than six months old. Beef comes mainly from bullocks (male animals) because the females are needed for milk. Pork and bacon come from different types of pig – pork pigs tend to be short and fat. Bacon pigs are long and thin.

Meat is made up of long, thin muscle fibres held together with connective tissue. Some cuts of meat are tougher than others. Cuts of meat like shin beef come from the part of the animal that does a lot of work (i.e. the leg, in this case). For this reason, shin beef needs long, slow cooking like stewing. Other cuts of meat (e.g. fillet, sirloin or rump steak) can be cooked quickly because the muscle fibres are shorter.

ACTIVITY

Suggest a different cooking method for each of the cuts of meat listed below. The cooking methods are given for you to choose from.

Meat: Pork chops, leg of lamb, pork fillet, neck of lamb chops, sirloin steak.

Methods: Stewing, frying, roasting, grilling, stir-frying.

Checking the temperature of meat

Meat and poultry can carry bacteria that can cause food poisoning. They must be stored away from cooked foods. Frozen meat and poultry must be defrosted thoroughly before cooking. Take care when cooking meat and poultry – remember they are high-risk foods. Lamb and duck can be served 'pink' and beef can be served 'rare'. All other meat and poultry should be thoroughly cooked.

Fish

There are three types of fish:

- oily – salmon, tuna, sardines, mackerel, etc.
- white – cod, haddock, whiting, plaice, sole, coley, etc.
- shellfish – prawns, shrimps, scampi, crabs, mussels, oysters, etc.

The flesh of fish is made up of muscle and connective tissue. Because the muscles are short and the connective tissue is very thin, fish cooks very quickly. Fish of all types 'go off' quickly, so it is important to carry out quality checks. Fish should smell slightly salty or like the sea, it should have firm flesh, bright red gills and clear eyes with plenty of scales. Shellfish must have tightly closed shells and a fresh smell.

Fish is great to cook with because it cooks quickly and can be used in many different dishes. Remember to store it in the fridge until it is needed. Shellfish is a high-risk food so should be eaten on the day it is bought. Tinned (canned) fish is a very good alternative to fresh fish and provides excellent food value.

ACTIVITY

Match the fish in the list to the correct dish. You may need to use a recipe book, or ask your teacher to help.

Plaice	Chowder
Clams	Moules marinières
Tinned salmon	Rollmops
King prawns	Battered fish with chips
Cod	Kedgeree
Smoked haddock	Fish goujons
Herrings	Kebabs
Mussels	Fishcakes

Pasta, rice and other cereals

The main cereals are wheat, rice, corn, oats, barley and rye. They can be used as:

- grains – whole or crushed
- flour – to make pasta, bread, cakes, pastries, biscuits, etc.
- breakfast cereals – Shredded Wheat, Rice Krispies, cornflakes, porridge, etc.

Flour is used extensively in the catering industry. Different varieties of wheat produce different flours. Strong wheat has a high protein (gluten) content and produces strong flour, used for making pasta and bread. Weak wheat has a low protein (gluten) content and produces soft flour that is used for making ordinary baked goods like cakes, pastry and biscuits.

ACTIVITY

What type of flour would you use for:

- iced buns?
- wholemeal bread rolls?
- short-crust pastry?
- Swiss roll?
- fairy cakes?
- scones?

Rice and pasta make excellent alternatives to potatoes. Dried pastas, in particular, have all the advantages of rice. They:

- are cheap to buy
- are easy to obtain
- are easy to store
- have a long shelf life
- cook quickly
- have good nutritional value
- can be used in a number of different ways
- come in a variety of types.

ACTIVITY

Pasta comes in many different shapes and sizes, e.g. spaghetti and ravioli. Name and describe six other shapes.

Rice is the grain of a cultivated grass. Chefs use different varieties of rice depending on the dish they are making. Short-grain rice 'clumps' together when cooked. Pudding rice (used for rice pudding) and arborio rice (used for risottos) are examples of short-grain rice. Long-grain rice remains fluffy, firm and separate when cooked, so is popular in dishes such as curry. Examples of long-grain rice are Carolina and basmati. Brown rice gives more food value than white rice but has a long cooking time. Wild rice is another grass that has a high nutritional value. It is expensive but makes food look attractive. It is sometimes mixed with other rice.

Fruit and vegetables

These are very useful in cookery because of their colour, flavour, texture and versatility. They are high in nutrients. Government nutritionists recommend that everyone should eat at least five portions a day of fruit and vegetables.

Fruit is best eaten fresh if possible. but other forms are useful additions to a balanced diet. Fruit can be:

- dried, e.g. dates, figs, currants, sultanas, raisins, apples, bananas, prunes
- canned (tinned), e.g. mandarin oranges, pears, peaches, pineapple and mixed fruits (e.g. fruit cocktail)
- frozen, e.g. apples, blackcurrants, raspberries, strawberries, mixed fruits
- made into juice, e.g. oranges, apples, pineapples, blackcurrants, mixed tropical fruits, mixed citrus fruits, cranberries
- made into jam/preserves, e.g. strawberries, raspberries, apricots, damsons, plums, mixed fruits, citrus fruits for marmalade, mango for mango chutney
- glacé (preserved in heavy sugar syrup), e.g. cherries
- crystallised (whole fruits preserved in sugar), e.g. peaches, mandarins, cherries
- candied (preserved in sugar), e.g. orange and lemon peel (mixed peel).

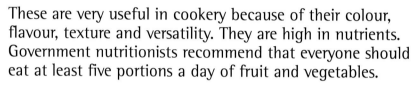

ACTIVITY

Name a different dish that you could prepare with each of the following types of fruit: frozen apples, glace cherries, orange juice, tinned pineapples, sultanas, apricot jam.

Vegetables are traditionally used for savoury dishes, while fruits are used for sweet dishes. The 'fruits' of a plant always contain the seeds, stone or pips of a new plant (with a few exceptions, e.g. rhubarb). Vegetables can come from any part of a plant. If you picture a vegetable in your mind it will help you identify which part of the plant you are preparing and eating.

Here are some examples of types of vegetables;

- roots – carrots, parsnips, turnips, beetroot
- tubers – potatoes and Jerusalem artichokes
- bulbs – onions, shallots, garlic
- stems – asparagus, celery
- leaves – cabbage, lettuce, spinach, Brussels sprouts, spring greens
- flowers – cauliflower, broccoli
- seeds – peas, beans, sweetcorn
- fungi – mushrooms.

Peppers, tomatoes, courgettes, cucumber, marrow are all actually fruits, but we refer to them as vegetables and use them in savoury dishes.

One of the most important skills you will learn in catering is how to prepare standard vegetable cuts. Practice is essential in order to gain this skill. Good luck!

ACTIVITY

Practise chopping vegetables into the standard vegetable cuts, then check them against the diagrams below.

1. Julienne (matchsticks)
2. Brunoise (tiny dice cut from julienne)
3. Jardinière (batons)
4. Macédoine (medium dice)
5. Paysanne (triangles, circles, squares, crescents)

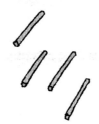

| Julienne | Brunoise | Jardinière | Macédoine | Paysanne |

Eggs

We can eat eggs from hens, turkeys, geese, ducks, guinea fowl, quail and gulls. The most commonly used are hens' eggs. They are graded in four sizes: small, medium, large and very large. The size of the egg only affects the price, not the quality. We can get free-range or battery eggs. When buying eggs you should look for:

- clean, well-shaped eggshells
- a high proportion of thick egg white to thin egg white when the egg is broken (a lot of thin egg white means the egg is old)
- yolks that are firm, round and an even colour.

Eggs are high in protein and they provide energy, fat, minerals and vitamins. They should be stored in a cool place. The shells are porous and will absorb strong flavours, so they should be kept away from strong-smelling foods like onions. They can be fried, scrambled, poached, boiled or used in omelettes and a range of other dishes such as quiche.

Eggs are extremely versatile and can also be used in a variety of other ways:

- whisked – Swiss roll, sponge flan or gateau
- as a glaze – pastry dishes e.g. sausage rolls or pasties
- to set a mixture – quiche
- to bind – fish cakes
- to coat – fish cakes, chicken joints, scotch eggs
- to emulsify – mayonnaise.

Dairy products

Milk

Milk is valued as a 'complete' food because it contains nearly all the nutrients that we need for health. It is a very important part of diets in the UK. Most of the milk we drink in the UK comes from cows, but it can also come from sheep, goats, camels and horses. Vegetable milk comes from plants, nuts or beans, e.g. soya milk.

Milk comes in a variety of forms:

- whole (full-fat)
- semi-skimmed (half-fat)

- skimmed (low-fat)
- ultra heat treated (UHT)
- sterilised
- evaporated
- condensed
- dried
- vegetable milk, e.g. coconut milk, soya milk.

Milk products

There is a wide range of products made from milk. These include cream, butter, cheese, yoghurt and dairy ice cream.

Cream

Different creams have different properties. Some are used for pouring, some for whipping and some for spooning. It is important that you select the correct type of cream to use when cooking. The 'thickness' of cream depends on its fat content, e.g. single or pouring cream contains 18 per cent fat whereas clotted cream used for spooning contains 55 per cent fat.

Popular types of cream are single cream, whipping cream, double cream and clotted cream. Long-life cream is available in cartons and spray cans. Both are popular in the catering industry.

Cake decorated with whipped cream

Butter

Butter is made from cream, as many people will know if they have whisked their cream too enthusiastically!

Butter can be salted or unsalted. Indian cookery uses *ghee*, a type of clarified butter, which is available commercially. Many caterers use flavoured butters to serve with foods like fish and steaks, e.g. parsley butter, herb butter, garlic butter, anchovy butter.

Yoghurt

There are a number of types of yoghurt available for the caterer to use. They include whole milk varieties, low-fat varieties, bio-yoghurt, French set, Greek yoghurt and fromage frais. Yoghurt is also available frozen.

Dairy ice cream

Dairy ice cream is made from a mixture of whole milk, cream, eggs and sugar. Most ice cream sold in the UK is made with a mixture of water, fat, sugar and milk powder. Ice cream desserts are extremely popular in restaurants, particularly with children.

Cheese

Cheese can be made from cows' or goats' milk. Most cheeses made in the UK are from cows' milk. Cheese is high in protein. It is also high in fat. Cheese can be hard, soft or blue veined. It should be stored in a cool place and wrapped. Buy cheese in small quantities as it doesn't keep for long.

Cheese can be eaten raw and there is very little, if any, waste. Some types have a wax coating that needs to be cut off. Cheese is fairly cheap, has good flavour and can be used in cooking, e.g. sauces, cheesecakes, pasties.

 ACTIVITY

List as many cheeses as you can think of in the following categories:

- hard
- soft
- blue.

Describe six different ways of using cheese in cooking.

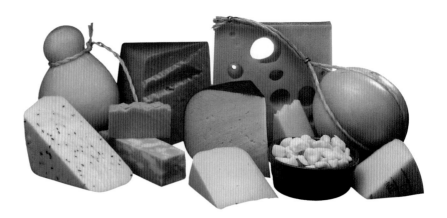

Vegetable protein

Some people prefer not to eat produce from an animal and use alternatives such as textured soya (mince or pieces), quorn or tofu. Textured soya is a protein made from wheat and soya beans. It can also be used as a meat extender: it can be used to replace as much as 60 per cent of meat in products such as meat pies. Quorn is produced from a plant derived from the mushroom family and can also be used as an alternative to meat; it does not shrink in cooking and can take on the flavour from the other ingredients it is cooked with. Tofu is made from soya beans and can be used in stir-fries and other dishes. It is high in protein.

Tofu with mushrooms and salad

Sauces

A sauce is a liquid that has been thickened.

The usual ways of thickening sauces are by using:

- a roux – equal quantities of fat and flour
- cornflour or arrowroot – blended to a paste with liquid
- beaten egg yolks.

A good sauce should be smooth, shiny and well seasoned. Sauces are used for many reasons. Here are some of the main ones. They:

- add colour
- add flavour/taste – especially to insipid (tasteless) food
- add texture
- bind (stick) foods together
- improve appearance or presentation of food
- add food value
- counteract (take away) the richness of some foods.

Sauces have different consistencies, depending on what they are being used for. A pouring sauce would be used for custard to accompany apple pie. A coating sauce would be used for cheese sauce to 'coat' cauliflower or macaroni. A really thick sauce called a 'panada' would be used to bind together the ingredients for fish cakes or meat balls.

Hot and cold desserts

There are many types of hot and cold desserts. Desserts can be made to suit all needs and tastes. Here are some examples:

- Egg-based desserts include crème caramel, bread-and-butter pudding and baked egg custard. In these dishes the eggs coagulate to enable the dessert to set.
- Steamed puddings are quite stodgy and heavy. They include jam roly-poly, treacle sponge and Christmas pudding. Traditionally they were served with custard, but can also be served with a sweet sauce or ice cream.
- Meringue-based products include Pavlova, vacherin and baked Alaska.
- Milk puddings can be eaten hot or cold and include baked rice pudding or semolina.

Desserts can be served with a range of sweet sauces including custard, almond sauce, Melba sauce, rum sauce or brandy butter.

Pastry products can be made from convenience mixes such as short crust. Using these products gives the chef more time to produce more dishes. You can also buy frozen pastry, such as short-crust or puff pastry, suitable for making a range of desserts. Pastry desserts include apple pie, profiteroles, lemon meringue pie, fruit tartlets and cream horns.

A lot of desserts include fresh fruit and can look very appealing to the eye. Although they may be high in fat and sugar it is possible to reduce these by using low-calorie sweeteners and unsaturated fats to meet the needs of those trying to live a healthier lifestyle.

ACTIVITY

List five dishes that can be made with whisked eggs.

List five different types of pastry.

Name four hot puddings that are baked.

List six cold desserts using pastry.

Find a recipe for ice cream and have a go at making it.

Try the traditional way of cooking a steamed sponge pudding in a saucepan of water.

Basic dough products

Dough products are made from a basic bread dough containing yeast. To make basic bread dough, you should use strong plain flour as it contains more gluten. Gluten is a sticky protein found in wheat and other grains. When mixed with water, it becomes stretchy and helps the products to rise. The yeast in the dough is activated with warm water. It is killed by excess heat, and if this happens the dough will not rise. You can use quick-acting dried yeast or fresh yeast to make dough. Fresh yeast is not always available and dried yeast can be stirred straight into the flour, it does not need to be mixed with water first. Oil or fat is added to keep the dough fresh, but it is not essential. Salt is also added to give the dough more flavour.

Kneading the dough helps to stretch the gluten so that the dough can rise and keep its shape. It can be done by hand or machine, using a dough hook. A food processor can also be used for small quantities. The dough should then be left to rise in a warm place. It should be loosely covered to prevent a hard skin forming. The dough should be baked in a hot oven Gas 8, 230°C – the heat makes the bread rise a little more before killing the yeast, and the bread then sets and holds its shape. The bread can be brushed with beaten egg and milk to give it a glazed finish. To test if bread is ready, tap the bottom. If it sounds hollow it is cooked.

A basic bread dough can be shaped in many ways, e.g. loaf, plait or knot. Toppings such as seeds or cheese can be added to give the dough more flavour and texture. Ingredients can be added to the dough to give it more flavour, such as currants, herbs or garlic.

ACTIVITY

Find out the names of a variety of breads from four other countries.

Make a sweet product from a basic bread dough.

Make a flavoured dough and shape it. How does it change during cooking?

> **ACTIVITY**
>
> Fill in the missing words to show how to make a basic dough.
>
> Mix _____ and fat in a bowl. In a jug, mix _____ , salt and _____ together. Gradually add _____ mixture to _____ to form a soft, but not sticky dough.
>
> _____ until smooth, _____ and leave to rise. Cook at Gas 8, 230°C until bread is firm and brown. If the bottom sounds _____ when tapped, the bread is ready.

Cakes, sponges, scones and biscuits

There are four different methods of making cakes, sponges, scones and biscuits:

- the rubbing-in method
- creaming
- whisking
- melting.

The rubbing-in method is used for cakes, scones, pastry and some biscuits. It is used for cakes that do not have a large amount of fat compared to flour, e.g. rock buns which have 75g fat and 200g flour.

- The fat is cut into chunks (block margarine is best) and, using the fingertips, is rubbed into the flour to form crumbs.
- Any optional ingredients (e.g. sultanas) are then added before the liquid or egg that binds the crumbs together.
- The mixture is baked in a fairly hot oven, Gas 5 or 6 (190°–200°C). The cakes will only keep fresh for a short time as they do not contain a lot of fat.

The creaming method is used for cakes that contain more fat and sugar compared to flour, such as sponge cakes. These cakes will last longer as they have more fat than those made using the rubbing-in method.

- The fat and sugar are creamed together using a wooden spoon. The eggs and flour are then added and mixed to make a light and fluffy mixture.
- Self-raising flour is used to make the cakes rise and so there is no need to add baking powder.

- It is better to use soft margarine for these cakes as it is easier to cream. Caster sugar has smaller crystals than granulated, so it mixes better. Flavourings such as cocoa can be added to the mixture.
- The eggs should be at room temperature.
- These cakes are cooked at a lower temperature, Gas 4 or 5 (180°–190°C) for 20–25 minutes.

The whisking method is used for making light sponge cakes. This type of cake does not contain any fat, so does not keep well.

- The eggs and sugar are whisked together until they are light and you can form a figure eight on top.
- The self-raising flour is sieved and folded into the mixture gently using a metal spoon. This must be done a little at a time to prevent pockets of flour forming.
- The mixture is then put into the prepared tins and cooked at Gas 6 (200°C) for 10–12 minutes. The mixture is very light and flexible making it ideal to roll when warm.
- It can be decorated in a variety of ways with fresh cream and fruit.

The melting method is used less often than the other methods. The fat and syrup are melted in a pan and poured into the other ingredients. The mixture is very wet and these cakes often improve in flavour if kept a little.

ACTIVITY

List four cakes that can be made using the rubbing-in method.

Try making a cake using the creaming method.

Make and decorate a gateau using the whisking method.

Find three recipes for cakes using the melting method. Put these recipes into your recipe file to try at a later date.

REMEMBER

Remember, some biscuit mixtures will spread when cooking so leave a space around the mixture. Grease the tray well to prevent the biscuits from sticking.

Scones and biscuits are often made using the rubbing-in or creaming methods. Scones are easy to make and take only a short time to cook. As they do not contain a lot of fat, they should be eaten soon after being made. Scones should be light, well risen and golden brown. The scone dough should be soft not sticky, the scones should be 2 cm thick before they are put in the oven and they should be cooked

> **Basic ingredients for shortbread:**
>
> 150g plain flour
> 100g butter
> 50g caster sugar
>
> Then try one of these ingredients instead:
> – self-raising flour or wholemeal flour
> – half butter, half lard or all lard
> – brown sugar.

at the top of a hot oven. Do not over handle the scone mix as it will make the scones heavy and hard.

Biscuits are easy to make at home and have a better flavour than shop-bought biscuits. You should always leave the biscuits on the tray to cool after cooking, as this will give them time to set a little. Biscuits do not set until they are cool, so don't leave them in the oven until they are crisp.

ACTIVITY

Find a recipe for biscuits using the creaming method and another using the rubbing-in method. Try them out and compare the results.

Make sweet and savoury scones.

Make shortbread biscuits, using the basic ingredients listed in the box. Then change the ingredients to see what happens. Compare your results as a class.

Pastry making

Many types of pastry are used in the catering industry. Different pastries can be used to produce dishes with a wide range of textures and flavours. The most common types of pastry are:

- short paste – short-crust pastry used for sweet and savoury dishes, e.g. mince pies and quiche Lorraine
- sugar paste – paté sucré, used for sweet dishes, e.g. lemon meringue pie
- cheese pastry – used for cheese straws and savoury flans
- choux pastry – used for éclairs and profiteroles
- puff pastry – used for sweet and savoury dishes, e.g. cream horns and sausage rolls
- rough puff pastry, used in the same way as puff pastry
- flaky pastry, used in the same way as puff pastry
- filo pastry – used for sweet and savoury dishes, e.g. strudel.

Short-crust pastry is the best-known pastry used and is made by the rubbing-in method. Experienced chefs get to know the 'feel' of the rubbed-up mixture and are accurate when adding the water so that their pastry is 'short', i.e. crisp and light.

Rubbing in   **Adding water**   **Gathering the dough**

Top tips for perfect short crust pastry:

- Keep everything as cool as possible, i.e. use fats straight from the refrigerator.
- Sieve the flour to aerate it (add air) as well as get rid of lumps.
- Use a mixture of fats, unless making vegetarian pastry. Lard gives pastry its short texture and margarine gives it colour and flavour. Measure the fats accurately – no more than half the weight of the flour.
- Rub in with fingertips only – these are the coolest parts of the hand so the pastry is less likely to go sticky. Lift your hands above the bowl as you are rubbing in to aerate the mixture and keep it cool.
- Once the mixture looks like breadcrumbs and is a sandy texture, i.e. feels like damp sand – stop rubbing!
- Add the correct amount of water, which is 1 teaspoon of water to every 25g flour (this equals 2 tablespoons for 150g flour) and 'cut it' into the rubbed up mixture with a palette knife.
- Once mixture starts to 'clump' together, use your hand to gather and stick the dough together.
- Knead pastry dough very lightly into the shape you want, i.e. a round shape for a round flan tin.
- Roll the pastry as evenly as possible, working parallel to the front and back of the table – do not turn the pastry over.
- Cut out the required shapes or use pastry to line a flan tin, dish, etc.
- Always push pastry into shape of dish – never stretch pastry.
- Allow to 'rest' before baking.
- Use a hot oven for pastry so that the fat melts and sets into the pastry quickly (Gas mark 6 or 200°C is the usual temperature for pastry items).

Students often struggle when rolling out this pastry, as they tend to over-handle it. A good tip is to place the pastry between two sheets of greaseproof paper (making a pastry 'sandwich') and then roll it out. It stops over-handling and the pastry instantly becomes more manageable.

Paté sucré

This is a sweet pastry, which is much softer to handle – but it can be moulded. It tastes delicious and is worth the extra effort it takes to make!

Savoury pie

Sweet pie

Comparison of short-crust pastry and paté sucré

Short-crust pastry	Paté sucré
Recipe: 150g plain flour 75g fat (mixture of margarine and lard) 2 tbs cold water	Recipe: 150g plain flour 100g margarine 1 egg yolk 1–2 tbs caster sugar
Method: Sieve flour into bowl. Cut and then rub fats into flour to form a sandy texture. Add water to form a dough.	Method: Sieve flour into bowl. Cut and then rub margarine into flour until a sandy texture is formed. Separate egg – lightly beat together the egg yolk and sugar. Add egg mixture to flour and fat to form a dough. Wrap and allow to chill before using.
Uses Savoury dishes, e.g. savoury pies, quiche, savoury flan, sausage rolls. Sweet dishes, e.g. fruit pies, mince pies, Bakewell tart, lemon meringue pie.	Uses Sweet dishes only, e.g. fruit pies, mince pies, Bakewell tart, lemon meringue pie.

Choux pastry

Choux pastry is used to make éclairs and profiteroles. Choux pastry is made in a very different way to other pastries although the basic ingredients of flour, margarine, water and egg are still used.

Tips for making choux pastry:

- Measure all ingredients accurately before starting to work and sieve the flour onto a plate.
- Ensure paste forms a soft ball in the pan.
- Cool to blood heat before adding eggs.

- Add eggs a little at a time and beat well.
- Preheat oven.
- When cooked, pastry should sound 'crisp' when lifted off and dropped back onto baking tray.
- Release steam by piercing pastry.

Choux pastry

Convenience products

The use of convenience foods is now well established in the UK. A convenience food is one where some or all of the preparation is already done – hence the word 'convenient'.

Why are convenience foods popular with caterers?

They are popular because they:

- save the time which would be spent preparing fresh alternatives
- may save money – foods out of season are often cheaper in convenience form than fresh foods
- may generate fewer air miles – some hotels spend money on fresh foods that are out of season and have to be imported
- have a long shelf life, leading to less food wastage
- are often quick to prepare and cook
- always taste the same – consistent quality
- are easy to use even for inexperienced chefs
- are easy to store – especially dried and canned foods
- are good as a 'stand-by' in case of emergencies.

The following chart shows caterers which convenience products to use.

Chart of convenience products

Type	Packaged items (where food is cooked or prepared)	Beverages	Packaged items (where food is not cooked or fully prepared)
Full convenience	butter portions jam portions sliced bread potted shrimps gâteaux salad dressings	fruit juices	frozen fruit
Pre-service convenience	ice cream canned fruit canned meats canned soup fruit pies	tea bags liquid coffee	frozen fruit
Pre-cooking convenience	canned steak dehydrated soup sausage rolls fish fingers croquettes		uncooked frozen pies/pastries breadcrumbed scampi scallops portioned meat/suprêmes of chicken
Pre-assembly convenience	canned steak frozen pastry fruit pie fillings pastry products	ground coffee	sponge mixes pastry mixes unfrozen scampi fish fillets/portioned meat
Basic convenience		coffee beans (to be ground)	peeled vegetables dried fruit jointed meats minced meat, sausages

Source: J. Campbell, D. Foskett and V. Ceserani, *Practical Cookery*, 11th edn, Hodder Education, 2008.

What types of convenience foods are there?

Convenience foods include:

- fresh convenience, e.g. sliced bread, ready-made cakes and pastries
- canned, e.g. baked beans, canned fruit, canned soup, canned meat
- dried, e.g. dried fruit, powder milk, pasta, rice

- frozen, e.g. pies, breaded scampi, frozen fruit, frozen pastry
- chilled, e.g. coleslaw, cook-chill dishes, pâté
- vacuum packed, e.g. fruit, vegetables, meat
- portion controlled foods, e.g. butter portions, jam portions.

Caterers have to assess what convenience products to use. This may depend on the time that is available, how much money they have to spend, the skill of the chefs, the equipment that is available and the type of food service they offer.

Methods of cooking

Why do we cook food?

- To make food easier to digest.
- To add flavour to food.
- To make food look more appetising.
- To make food smell more appetising.
- To make food safer to eat (destroys bacteria).
- To prevent spoilage and increase keeping qualities.

What cooking does to food

All foods contain protein, fat, carbohydrates, vitamins, minerals and water. Animal proteins need to be broken down and vegetable proteins softened. Fats need other foods, such as vegetables or starchy food like bread, to enable the body to digest them more easily. The starchy carbohydrates in potatoes are indigestible in their raw state and have to be cooked first. Heating breaks down foods, bringing out the flavour and producing an appetising smell. However, heat can destroy important vitamins in food. For this reason, it is important to keep cooking times as short as possible and use the correct method of cooking.

Methods of heat exchange

Conduction: stir-frying with a wok

Convection: boiling potatoes in hot water

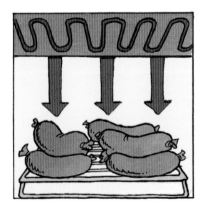

Radiation: grilling

All of these methods are used in transferring heat to food in the cooking process. Sometimes convection and conduction work together in order to exchange heat, e.g. the surface of a baked potato is heated by convection, then the heat is conducted through to the centre of the potato.

Cooking methods

The three main methods of cooking are:

- cooking in water
- cooking in fat
- cooking in an oven.

Cooking in water

Have you ever heard the joke about people who can't even boil an egg? The important thing about cooking is to make sure you are familiar with your cooker and hob so that you get used to which setting gives which degree of heat! This sounds easy, until you try it ...

Boiling

Boiling is cooking in deep, bubbling liquid in an open or covered pan. Foods can be boiled in water, stock or wine. In the catering industry, boiling pans and bratt pans can be used for boiling. When food is boiled, starches are softened, proteins are broken down and water-soluble vitamins are leached into the liquid.

When deciding whether to place foods into boiling or cold water the rule is:

- All root vegetables (those grown in the ground) have a cold-water start.
- All other vegetables, plus rice, pasta and eggs have a hot-water start.

Simmering

Simmering is cooking in deep water just below boiling point. When food is simmered, starches are softened, proteins are broken down but water-soluble vitamins are largely preserved. Simmering is used for foods like dumplings, rice, egg dishes and fruit.

Steaming

Poaching eggs

A pressure cooker

Blanching

Steaming

Steaming is cooking in a perforated container over boiling water, although the modern combination (combi) ovens and pressure-less steamers used in the catering industry steam very effectively.

Steaming is an excellent method of cooking, as the steam cannot flush out the nutrient content of the food. Food also retains its shape and more of its natural flavour.

Steaming is used for vegetables, potatoes, steamed puddings, fish and tender pieces of meat. Steaming is a great way to reheat food without spoiling it.

Poaching

Poaching is lengthy steaming with the liquid off the boil. Eggs need gentle poaching so that the white stays intact.

Pressure-cooking

Pressure-cooking is cooking in a sealed pan. The higher the pressure – the shorter the cooking time. Pressure steamers are used in the catering industry to deliver a constant supply of vegetables and puddings for busy service times.

Remember: Always follow the manufacturer's instructions when using a pressure cooker – doors or lids must not be opened until the pressure has been released.

Stewing

Stewing is cooking food in its own juices in a covered pan. If food has a low water content, more liquid needs to be added for the cooking process. Stewing is a long, slow method of cooking, used to tenderise tough cuts of meat and to cook delicate vegetables and fruit.

Blanching

Blanching is short cooking in boiling liquid. The short cooking time prevents the enzymes that destroy vitamins and minerals from becoming active. Chefs often blanch vegetables and then plunge them into cold water to halt the cooking process. These vegetables can then be reheated very quickly for food service without losing their colour or shape.

Bain-marie or water bath

This is a very gentle cooking process carried out by standing the food in a container (bain-marie or water bath) either suspended in or standing in hot but not boiling water. It is used for cooking delicate foods like egg custards or sauces containing high percentages of butter, eggs or cream that would separate or burn with direct heat.

In food service areas, e.g. a cafeteria service counter, a bain-marie is used for 'hot-holding' food.

A bain-marie

Cooking in fat

The important thing to remember about frying is that you are cooking at twice the temperature of cooking in water and a single minute can mean the difference between perfectly cooked food and a disaster!

Shallow frying

Shallow frying is a quick method of cooking in which food is browned in hot fat. All foods should be turned and cooked and browned on both sides. As a general rule, the 'presentation side' of the food (the side that the customer will see on the plate) should always be fried first as this side will have the best appearance.

Sautéing

Literally translated from the French, this means 'jump or toss'. Sautéing is tossing small pieces of food in fat that is hot but not smoking. Ideally this is carried out in a pan with a handle (a sauté pan is ideal). A mixture of oil and butter is considered to be best for sautéing. Foods such as fish, liver, kidney and strips of steak are ideal for sautéing.

Deep-frying

Deep-frying is cooking food in a friture or deep-fat fryer, in deep fat. It is important that the food is able to float freely in the fat. Because of the safety issues of using hot fat there are some rules you should follow when using a deep-fat fryer.

Safety when frying

- Use a good quality oil.
- Never fill friture (deep-fat fryer) more than three-quarters full.
- Dry food thoroughly before frying.
- Do not fry too much food at once.
- Normal frying temperature should be between 175°C and 195°C.
- Allow the fat to 'recover' its heat before adding more food.
- Strain fat after use.
- Have frying basket and spider to hand for safety.
- Protect delicate foods with batter, flour, egg and breadcrumbs or pastry to prevent breaking up in the hot fat.
- Change fat regularly.

Stir-frying

Stir-fried food is stirred and tossed very quickly in a deep pan or wok using a very small amount of oil. The success of stir-frying relies on excellent preparation of the food. As large a surface area as possible is exposed, so the food cooks as soon as it goes into the pan or wok. Stir-frying is very popular in the preparation of Chinese dishes.

Braising

This is a method of cooking used for inexpensive cuts of meat. It is a combination of frying, steaming and stewing. A selection of vegetables is fried and placed in the bottom of a dish. A (browned) joint of meat is placed on top and liquid is added to come half-way up the food. The dish is covered and cooked slowly inside an oven. The fat gives the food a delicious brown crust and the juices can be used for gravy.

Flambéing

This is not a 'cooking' method in the traditional sense; but the term used to describe quick flaming of food in alcohol (usually brandy, rum or Calvados). Flambéing is used to give added flavour to food and usually follows shallow frying. Most of the alcohol burns off to leave only the flavour. High percentage alcohols (40 per cent proof) should be used.

Flambéing is carried out in high-class restaurants by trained staff when preparing dishes such as Crêpes Suzette and Steak Diane.

Fondue cookery

A fondue can be used as a container for hot fat. Small pieces of meat (usually veal, beef or pork) are dipped into the fondue on long skewers to cook and served with sauces, salads and bread.

A fondue with cheese

Cooking in an oven

Cooking in an enclosed space is one of the oldest cooking methods known. Modern technology enables caterers to use convection ovens, combination ovens, microwave ovens and grills.

Heat can come from the sides, base or top of an oven. In a traditional oven, hot air rises so that the top shelf is always the hottest. Fan-assisted ovens, however, are the same temperature on every shelf.

Other types of oven used in a catering kitchen:

- baking oven or pastry oven
- forced air circulation (convection) oven
- combination (convection and steam) oven
- pizza oven
- proving oven.

Baking

Baking is cooking food in the dry heat inside an oven at temperatures between 100°C and 250°C or Gas ½ – 9. Baked goods usually have a good colour and texture. Baking is used for cakes, puddings, fish, pastry dishes, bread, potatoes and meat.

Below is an oven temperature guide for some baked foods.

Oven temp.	Gas mark	Foods to be cooked
160°C	4	Biscuits
180°C	5	Cakes and puddings
200°C	6	Shortcrust pastry
210°C	7	Puff pastry, bread, scones

Roasting

This is cooking and browning with the aid of fat. It can be carried out on a constantly revolving spit, e.g. a hog roast or spit-roast chicken, or in the oven. Roasting is a very popular method for cooking large pieces of meat such as those offered in carvery restaurants.

Casseroling

This is similar to braising. Food to be casseroled should be browned on the hob first as this quick browning 'seals' the meat to lock in the flavour. Once the liquid has been added to the casserole, cover and cook in a moderate oven.

Pot-roasting or casserole roasting

This is cooking seasoned meat either with or without a bed of root vegetables in a covered casserole or pan, using butter for basting. The lid of the casserole needs to be removed at the end of the cooking time to allow the meat to brown.

Grilling

Grilling is a method of cooking food under intense heat. Because it is such a quick method of cooking, the protein in food is broken down immediately so that no juices are lost. It is an excellent method of cooking for those on a diet to lose weight, as it uses no fat.

Expensive cuts of meat are needed because of the short cooking time, e.g. fillet steak, rump steak, sirloin steak, lamb cutlets, pork chops. Foods such as bacon, sausage, kidneys, tomatoes and mushrooms can also be grilled.

Tips for grilling

- Season food before grilling but add salt when cooked (salt draws out juices and makes meat dry)
- Pre-heat the grill for at least 3 minutes.
- Place food directly under the grill.
- Place thicker foods which take longer to cook lower down under the grill.

Cooking au gratin

Cooking au gratin is to brown dishes, e.g. foods in a cheese sauce, by intense heat from above.

Other types of grills used in catering

- A salamander is a type of 'top heat' grill used in many catering kitchens.
- A barbecue is popular for outside cooking. Barbecued food has a smoky flavour and should be seasoned or marinated before cooking. Always cook over glowing embers and not over flames. If very fatty food is barbecued, the fat will drip onto the charcoal and burn, producing thick smoke.
- A char-grill is similar to a barbecue as it 'holds' the food above the heat. Many fast food outlets use automatic conveyor char-grills to cook burgers and buns.
- With a rotary toaster, slices of bread are placed on a conveyor belt and are carried through the toaster until brown. Rotary toasters are used in many hotels where demand for toast is high, e.g. during breakfast service.

Microwaving

Microwave ovens cook or warm up food much quicker than a conventional oven. Microwaves quickly heat any food containing water, by causing the water to oscillate (vibrate), which produces heat. The food absorbs the microwaves, but the oven and the baking dish remain cool (depending on the length of cooking time).

Metals reflect microwaves and therefore metal dishes will cause sparks if they are used in a microwave. However, microwaves will pass through porcelain, earthenware, paper, cardboard, plastic, heat-resistant glass, and ceramic so any of these can be used.

Microwaves do not brown food, but special browning dishes can be used. Some microwave ovens combine convection with microwave power or a grill with microwave power.

Microwaves are primarily used for defrosting food and reheating pre-prepared foods. Microwaved food is popular because foods can be cooked without adding fat or water – an advantage for people on special diets.

Culinary terms

Culinary terms are often used in professional kitchens and in recipes. Some are used more often than others. Below are some of the terms you will be expected to know by the end of your course.

Term:	Meaning:
accompaniments	Items offered separately to main dish.
al dente	Firm to the bite.
au gratin	Sprinkled with cheese or breadcrumbs and browned.
bain-marie	A container of water to keep foods hot without fear of burning.
brûlée	Burned cream.
bouquet garni	A small bundle of herbs.
coulis	Sauce made of fruit or vegetable purée.
croûtons	Cubes of bread that are fried or grilled.
en croûte	In pastry.
entrée	Main course.
flambé	To cook with flame by burning away the alcohol.
garnish	Served as part of the main item, trimmings.
julienne	Thin, matchstick-size strips of vegetables.
marinade	A richly spiced liquid used to give flavour and assist in tenderising meat and fish.
mise-en-place	Basic preparation prior to assembling products.
purée	A smooth mixture made from food passed through a sieve.
reduce	To concentrate a liquid by boiling or simmering.
roux	A thickening of cooked flour and fat.
sauté	Tossed in fat.

TERMINOLOGY:

Mise-en-place – basic preparation prior to assembling products.

REMEMBER

Always complete your basic preparation prior to cooking and you will find your practical tasks much easier to complete.

Preparation is important!

Presenting food

The aim of a chef is to present food as near perfectly as possible. This involves taking into account:

- consistency (how thin or how thick)
- texture (includes crunchy, soft, crisp)
- flavour (includes salty, sweet, sour, bitter, well seasoned)
- seasoning (includes use of herbs, spices, salt and pepper)
- colour (remember white, cream, brown and green are 'dead' colours)
- decoration (used on sweet dishes – includes chocolate, cherries, fresh fruit, etc.)
- garnish (used on savoury dishes – includes tomato, parsley, lemon, cucumber, cress, etc.)
- accompaniments – these include colourful vegetables and sauces.

Chefs gradually learn the skills of tasting food to check for flavour, texture and seasoning.

Hot foods should be served hot and *not* warm, preferably on hot plates. Cold food should be served cold, but *not* frozen and always on cold plates. Food probes can be used to check temperatures.

Savoury food is usually served in oval dishes or on oval plates if appropriate (with plain doilies or dish-papers).

Sweet food is usually served in round dishes or on round plates if appropriate (with pretty doilies).

REMEMBER

As a general rule, do not over season, over-decorate or over-fill serving dishes.

Consistency

The consistency of food will depend on the size of pan used, the cooking time, the amount of thickener (e.g. flour) used and the quality of ingredients. It is easier to thin a mixture (like a soup or a sauce) rather than thicken it.

Texture

Tasting food is essential in order to test texture. This includes checking foods like rice, pasta (cooked al dente) and vegetables to ensure they are not over-cooked. Cooking alters the texture of food and an experienced cook will know when the right amount of heat has been applied to give the correct texture, for example when cooking steaks.

Contrasting textures are important to give variety and interest to a meal, for example croutons with soup, wafers and ice-cream, cheese and biscuits.

Flavour and seasoning

Taste is very important. Good chefs know how to retain the flavour of food and how to alter the flavour of food. To retain flavour, chefs need to:

- use food that is as fresh as possible
- use the least amount of cooking liquid
- use left-over cooking liquid where possible (for sauces, stocks and gravies)
- use appropriate cooking methods
- prepare, cook and serve in as short a time as possible
- avoid over-seasoning, so that the natural flavour comes through
- use herbs and strongly flavoured foods with care
- adjust seasoning at the end.

Nutrition links to healthy eating and menu planning.

Healthy eating is important at any age. Along with regular exercise, avoiding excess alcohol and stress and not smoking, a healthy diet can contribute to a healthy lifestyle.

Good nutrition is very important. It is needed for 'normal' growth and development. Once we mature we need to continue to eat well in order to maintain good health and fight off infections.

It is very rare to hear of starvation (severe lack of food) in the UK. However, there are serious health concerns about malnutrition (poor nutrition, i.e. eating the wrong type of food) which leads to dietary-related diseases such as obesity, anorexia, Type 2 diabetes, osteoporosis (brittle bone disease) and heart disease.

Nutrients

These are the chemicals found in food. The main nutrients are:

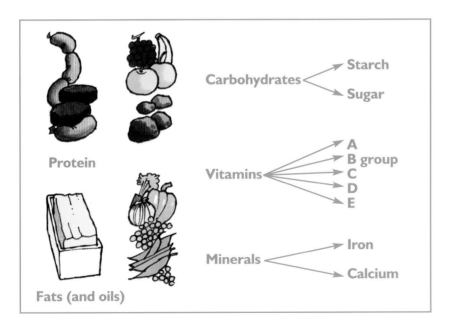

Water and fibre are also very important to include in the diet, but they are not classed as nutrients.

It is important to know which nutrients are in particular foods so that we can maintain a healthy diet.

What is a healthy balanced diet?

You may have heard of a 'balanced diet' but wondered what it really means. It does not mean eating the same amount of each food every day! It means eating a variety of foods each day, including foods from each of the four main food groups shown below.

Eating the recommended portions of the following food groups each day will help to make sure you get a balanced range of nutrients including the vitamins and minerals your body needs.

Meat and meat alternatives (e.g. fish, quorn, soya products)	2 portions
Milk and other dairy products	3 portions
Fruit and vegetables	5 portions
Potatoes and other starchy foods (e.g. rice, pasta, bread, cereals)	5–6 portions

A balanced diet
Try to eat wholegrain products when possible, e.g. wholemeal bread (instead of white bread), whole wheat cereals like Weetabix and Shredded Wheat (instead of sugar-coated cereals), and brown rice and pasta. Also try to cut down on fat, sugar and salt!

ACTIVITY

Plan a breakfast, lunch and evening meal suitable for a teenager, using the three empty plates below. Check to see you have the right number of portions from each food group!

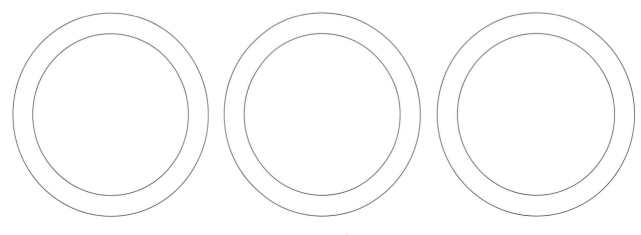

More about nutrients – the 'science bit'

Protein

Protein is the most important nutrient. This is because it is the only nutrient that can be used for **growth** (so especially important for children) and the **building and repair of body cells**. Protein is also known as the 'body-builder'.

Protein can come from animals (fish, meat and animal products like cheese, milk and eggs) or plants (peas, beans and lentils – sometimes called pulses, soya, nuts and cereals).

There are two types of protein – proteins of high biological value (HBV) and proteins of low biological value (LBV). Proteins are made up of amino acids. HBV proteins contain the essential amino acids. Ten essential amino acids are needed by children and eight are needed by adults. HBV proteins are found in fish, meat, cheese, milk, eggs and soya. LBV proteins are found in peas, beans, lentils, nuts and cereals.

Carbohydrates

Carbohydrates come from plants. They are the main 'energy providers'. They can be:

● starches, e.g. cereals, bread, pasta, rice, potatoes, etc., or
● sugars, e.g. sugar, honey, jams, marmalades, fruit, etc.

Fibre is sometimes classed as a carbohydrate – but more about that later!

Carbohydrates (starches and sugars) break down to simple sugars as they pass through the digestive system. Complex carbohydrates (such as whole grains) help maintain stable blood sugar levels. Too much sugary food in one go can affect blood sugar levels, making us feel energetic quickly, but then tired. Excess sugar is stored in muscle cells (to be ready for action) and in the liver. Unfortunately, if it is not used it is then stored as body fat.

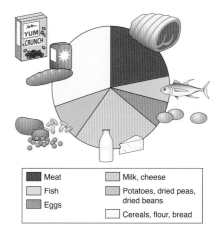

■ Meat	▨ Milk, cheese
▢ Fish	▨ Potatoes, dried peas, dried beans
▨ Eggs	▢ Cereals, flour, bread

Sources of protein

!P REMEMBER

Soya is the only plant-HBV protein. This is important to remember when planning meals for vegetarians and vegans.

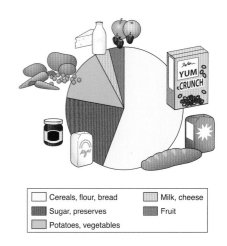

▢ Cereals, flour, bread	▨ Milk, cheese
■ Sugar, preserves	▨ Fruit
▨ Potatoes, vegetables	

Sources of carbohydrates

Good points about fats:

- They are needed to build cell membranes.
- They are needed to protect body organs, e.g. the kidneys.
- They 'lubricate' or 'grease' food to make it easier to swallow.
- They make you feel full for a long time.
- They form an 'insulating layer' under the skin to keep the body warm.
- They give food a lovely flavour.
- They give food a good texture, e.g. fried foods are often crisp.
- They contain the fat-soluble vitamins – particularly A and D.

Fats and oils

The first bit is easy to remember – fats are solid at room temperature and oils are liquid at room temperature.

Fats, like carbohydrates, are 'energy providers'. Because fats help to form an insulating layer under the skin they also give 'body warmth'. It is important to note that the same weight of fat gives twice as many calories as carbohydrates, so it is easy to eat too much! Although we hear a lot about how fat is 'bad for you', that's not quite true. Too much is bad for us, but our bodies need some fat for building cell membranes and for other jobs, like insulation.

However, we all need to make sure we don't eat too much fat. Too much fat can cause:

- obesity
- high cholesterol (fatty bits which clog the arteries)
- coronary heart disease (CHD)
- halitosis (bad breath)
- Type 2 diabetes.

Examples of fats include butter, margarine, lard and dripping. Examples of oils include corn oil, sunflower oil, peanut oil and sesame oil.

Vitamins

Vitamins are only needed in tiny amounts by the body, but as the name suggests, they are vital for good health.

The main vitamins are named after letters of the alphabet. They all have chemical names as well – but you don't need to remember them! Every vitamin has a specific job to do in the body so a lack of one particular vitamin can make you feel a bit 'under the weather'.

Vitamin A is needed to make 'visual purple' in the eye, which is needed to prevent 'night blindness'. It is also needed to keep our mucous membranes (like the tissues found in the nose) moist.

Vitamin B is not one vitamin but a group of vitamins that includes thiamine, niacin and riboflavin. They are needed to help release the energy from carbohydrate foods.

Vitamin C – does 'an apple a day keep the doctor away'? It's more likely to be an orange, some strawberries or blackcurrants! Vitamin C really is a vital vitamin. It is needed to make the connective tissue (a bit like glue) which holds body cells together. It also helps the body absorb iron. Have you ever wondered why visitors take fruit to people in hospital? Most accidents and operations involve loss of blood, so eating iron-rich foods with fruit containing vitamin C helps the body recover more quickly!

Vitamin D works with calcium to help form strong bones and teeth. Vitamin D is sometimes called the 'sunshine vitamin' because it can be manufactured (made) in the body by the action of sunlight on the skin. Don't overdo the sun though – burning can contribute to skin cancer.

Minerals

Gruesome fact: the mineral content of a body is all that is left after cremation, i.e. the ashes. Minerals are found in most foods and the only ones that might be lacking are calcium and iron. You need to know about these.

Iron is needed for making red blood cells. Blood is the body's transport system – it takes oxygen round the body to where it is needed. If there is not a good supply of red blood cells the transport system does not work very well. Lack of iron causes a disease called anaemia. This disease is more common in teenage girls and women because of monthly periods.

Calcium is needed for strong bones and teeth. Calcium works with vitamin D and phosphorus. Calcium also helps the blood to 'clot'. It is important that children have enough calcium because most 'bone mass' is laid down before the age of about 21. Lack of calcium could cause osteoporosis (brittle bone disease).

Water

Do you know how much of your body weight is water? The answer is approximately 65 per cent. The body can survive a long time without food but only a couple of days without water. This is because many body 'processes' need water.

Water is needed to:

- help control body temperature
- lubricate (grease) joints
- help digestion
- help remove waste products from the body.

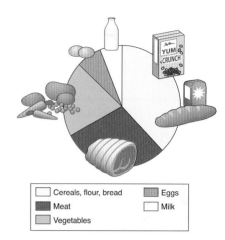

	Cereals, flour, bread		Eggs
	Meat		Milk
	Vegetables		

Sources of iron

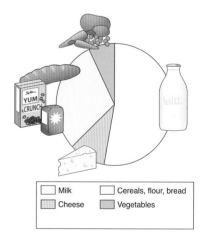

	Milk		Cereals, flour, bread
	Cheese		Vegetables

Sources of calcium

REMEMBER

Remember that eating foods rich in vitamin C will help the body absorb and make use of iron.

Adults need about 2½ litres of water a day. About 1½ litres comes from drinks. The rest comes from food. Fruits can be up to 90 per cent water – another good reason to eat five a day!

Fibre (NSP)

Fibre is also known by other names such as 'roughage' and 'non-soluble polysaccharides' (NSP) – what a mouthful! Fibre is not absorbed by the body – you can eat as much of it as you like and not put on any weight.

To understand why fibre is needed by the body, you need to imagine it passing through the body collecting all the rubbish and waste as it goes until it is finally 'expelled' from the body as faeces. As fibre passes through the body it absorbs water and bulks up the waste, making it soft. Lack of fibre can cause constipation.

If waste products stay in the intestines too long they can cause problems. Doctors think some cancers can be caused by lack of fibre and recommend that we eat 30g fibre a day. Fresh fruit and vegetables are high in fibre – yet another reason to eat five a day!

Malnutrition

Some diseases are caused by not having enough nutrients (starvation or under-nourishment) or by eating too much or too little of one or more nutrients (malnutrition).

 TERMINOLOGY:

Eat less sugar to prevent dental caries.

Eat less fat to prevent obesity.

Eat less fat to prevent coronary heart disease.

Eat less salt to prevent high blood pressure.

Eat more fibre to prevent constipation and bowel cancer.

 ACTIVITY

Look at the sentences below and fill in the blank spaces correctly, using a word from the following list: fat, carbohydrates, protein, vitamin A, vitamin B, vitamin C, vitamin D, iron, calcium, water, fibre.

Be careful – some nutrients are used more than once!

_____ is not a nutrient but is needed for healthy bowels and to avoid constipation.

Blood needs _____ to make red blood cells, which carry oxygen around the body to where it is needed.

Muscles in the body need _____ for work and physical activity.

_____ helps the body burn up energy foods.

Teeth need _____ and _____.

Two-thirds of your body weight is _____. It helps your body to function properly.

Eyes need _____.

Bones need _____ and _____.

Every cell of the body needs _____ for growth and repair.

The cells of the body must be held together. Body cells need _____ to be able to do this.

_____ is also needed to prevent illness.

_____ keeps the body warm and gives us energy. Too much _____ can cause obesity.

How does eating 'five a day' of fruit and veg fit into healthy eating guidelines?

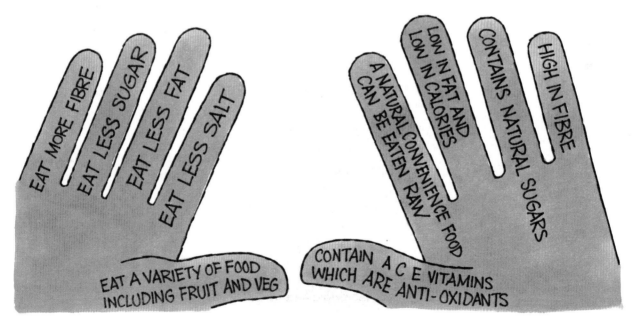

Healthy eating

EAT MORE FIBRE
EAT LESS SUGAR
EAT LESS FAT
EAT LESS SALT
EAT A VARIETY OF FOOD INCLUDING FRUIT AND VEG

'Five a day' fruit and veg

LOW IN FAT AND LOW IN CALORIES
A NATURAL CONVENIENCE FOOD CAN BE EATEN RAW
CONTAINS NATURAL SUGARS
HIGH IN FIBRE
CONTAIN A C E VITAMINS WHICH ARE ANTI-OXIDANTS

Healthy eating

We are what we eat, so we need to eat what is good for us!

Research has shown that there are links between what we eat and many modern diseases. For example:

- Heart disease may be caused by eating too much fat.
- Diabetes and tooth decay may be caused by eating too much sugar.
- High blood pressure and strokes may be caused by eating too much salt.
- Bowel cancer, constipation and diverticulosis may be caused by lack of fibre.
- Eating too much fat and sugar and too little fibre often causes obesity.
- Diabetes, high blood pressure, strokes and heart disease are also linked with obesity.

Eating too much or too little food, or the wrong type of food, are not the only reasons for poor health. Smoking, lack of exercise and drinking too much alcohol can also increase the risk of illness and early death.

Most of the calories we eat every day should come from complex carbohydrates such as bread, rice, pasta or potatoes. These foods are also low in fat and provide vitamins and minerals. When choosing protein foods, concentrate on low-fat sources such as lean meat, fish and poultry, e.g. chicken and turkey rather than full-fat dairy produce and fatty meat. Fruit and vegetables are a major source of vitamins and minerals and we should be eating at least five portions a day.

As well as knowing what to eat, we need to remember to cut down on fat, sugar, salt and alcohol.

Fat

The fat we eat comes from four main sources:

- meat and meat products
- fats used for spreading
- milk, cheese and cream
- cooking fats and oils.

There is also 'hidden' fat in chocolate, cakes, pastries, pies and other convenience foods.

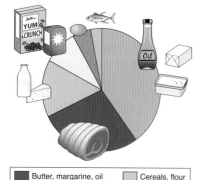

■ Butter, margarine, oil	▨ Cereals, flour
▨ Meat	▨ Eggs
▨ Milk, cheese	□ Fish

Sources of fats

As caterers it is important to cut down on the amount of fat we serve to our customers. Ways of achieving lower fat content include:

- cutting visible fat from meat
- choosing lean cuts of meat and offering smaller portions
- offering low-fat or polyunsaturated spreads, e.g. Flora, instead of or as well as butter
- using vegetable fats and oils rather than animal fats where possible
- cutting down the amount of fat used in recipes
- using lower-fat dairy products, e.g. skimmed or semi-skimmed milk, low-fat cheese, etc.
- cutting bread and chips thicker so there is less surface area for fat
- using soya products or Quorn as a substitute for meat
- using plain yogurt instead of cream
- offering oily fish, which are rich in Omega 3.

Sugar

In the UK we eat an average of 38kg of sugar per person every year! Less than half of this is bought as sugar. The rest is found in sweets, biscuits, cakes, sweet desserts and soft drinks. Sugar provides 'empty calories', i.e. calories without any other nutrients or goodness. Unfortunately, sugar tastes good and is quite addictive, so it is difficult to cut down.

As caterers we can reduce the amount of sugar we offer to our customers by:

- using sugar substitutes for puddings, cakes and biscuits when possible
- offering fresh fruit alternatives for dessert
- using tinned fruit in natural juices – not syrup
- offering low-calorie soft drinks.

Salt

On average we eat about 12g or two teaspoons of salt a day. Too much salt has been linked to high blood pressure, which is a risk factor for heart disease and strokes. Caterers can reduce the amount of salt they put in their customers' food by:

- reducing the amount of salt used in cooking
- using a salt substitute
- cutting down on the use of convenience foods
- cutting down on highly salted crisps, nuts and other nibbles.

Fibre

Dietary fibre is found in plant foods such as beans, grains and vegetables. Enzymes in the digestive system cannot digest some types of fibre, so they pass through the body unchanged. This is great news for people trying to maintain a healthy weight. Fibre fills you up and means you have less room for fatty, high-calorie foods.

Soluble fibre

Soluble fibre lowers cholesterol, helping to reduce the risk of heart disease. It also helps control the level of blood sugar by slowing down the rate at which food leaves the stomach (good news for diabetics). Soluble fibre is found in peas, beans and lentils and pectin-rich fruits like apples, cranberries and citrus fruits.

Lentil soup

Insoluble fibre

Insoluble fibre acts like a sponge; in other words, it expands to hold water and waste products as they pass through the intestines. Insoluble fibre helps to keep faeces (poo) soft so that you do not have to strain when going to the toilet. It also helps prevent constipation. Insoluble fibre is found in wholegrain, wholewheat and wholemeal cereals, e.g. All Bran.

Caterers can increase the amount of fibre they include in their dishes by:

- offering wholemeal bread and cereals
- offering wholewheat pasta and brown rice
- serving fruit and vegetables with the skin on
- serving fruit and vegetables raw if possible
- adding rolled oats to crumble toppings for extra fibre
- using wholemeal flour for pastry, cakes, biscuits, pancakes, etc.

Bran flakes

Fruit and vegetables – five a day

Healthy eating guidelines now include the fact that we should be eating a minimum of five portions of fruit and vegetables a day. We do not have to limit ourselves to fresh fruit and vegetables – frozen, canned and dried fruit and vegetables all count, as well as prepared salads, fruit juices, soups, vegetarian ready-meals and tomato-based pasta sauces.

To make the most of your 'five a day', it is recommended that we eat a 'rainbow' of different coloured fruit and vegetables in order to receive the full range of nutrients, particularly vitamins and minerals, that we need.

ACTIVITY

Make a list of at least three fruit and vegetables for each colour of the rainbow: red, orange, yellow, green, blue, indigo, violet.

There have been many guides to 'healthy eating'. These include the 'healthy eating pyramid', the 'eatwell plate' and the 'traffic light system'.

The eatwell plate

Use the eatwell plate to help you get the balance right. It shows how much of what you eat should come from each food group.

FOOD STANDARDS AGENCY
food.gov.uk

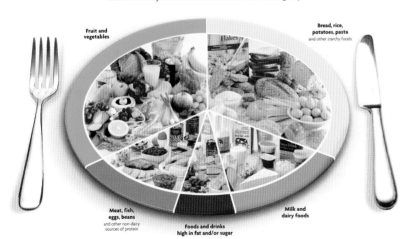

	Per serving
Fat	7.7g
Saturates	2.0g
Sugars	42.2g
Salt	2.0g
■ HIGH ■ MEDIUM ■ LOW	

Traffic light system

Healthy eating pyramid

The important thing to remember when planning meals is to include a wide variety of foods, particularly fresh fruit and vegetables, to ensure we get the vitamins and minerals that scientists know we need for good health.

Multi-cultural variations on healthy eating

Vegetarian diets

Some religions advocate a vegetarian diet. For some people, all life is valued and any food obtained by the suffering of animals is forbidden.

A vegetarian diet is considered healthy because of the emphasis on fresh fruit and vegetables. Protein is obtained mainly from beans, lentils, peas, nuts and wholegrain cereals, which are also rich in vitamins and minerals.

The 'Mediterranean' diet

Studies have shown that people who live in Mediterranean regions have long, healthy lives and do not suffer dietary related diseases to the same extent as people in the UK or America. Their diet is based on high levels of plant foods, including fruit, vegetables, pasta and beans. They eat a lot of fish and poultry and only a little red meat. They use only small amounts of processed foods.

Asian diets

People who eat traditional Asian diets are also at a lower risk of dietary related diseases than people who eat a typical western diet. Most of the calories come from plant-based foods, especially rice, which is the staple food of Asian countries. Meat is eaten in very small quantities.

Special diets

Some people choose not to eat certain foods. There can be a variety of reasons for this:

- because of their ethical beliefs
- because of their religious beliefs
- for medical reasons
- they do not like the taste or texture of some foods.

Vegetarian diets

There are many reasons why people choose a vegetarian diet:

- They may have strong feelings about the way animals are kept and slaughtered.
- Land used to feed animals could feed many more if used for crops.
- Many cases of food poisoning are linked to meat.
- A vegetarian diet is considered to be healthier (lower in fat and cholesterol, higher in fibre) than one that relies on meat.

A vegetarian dish

Many teenagers decide to become vegetarians.

There are three main categories of vegetarians:

1. Vegans do not eat the flesh of any animal (no meat, poultry or fish) and no eggs, milk, cheese, honey, etc.

2. Lacto-vegetarians do not eat the flesh of any animal (no meat, poultry or fish) but they do eat eggs, milk, cheese, honey, etc.

3. Demi- or semi-vegetarians often choose to eat a mainly vegetarian diet because they don't eat red meat. They sometimes do eat white meat (poultry and fish) and eggs, milk, cheese, honey, etc.

Religious diets

Different religions have different dietary restrictions. For example:

- Muslims do not eat pork (they believe the pig is an unclean animal). Meat has to be Halal (slaughtered in a special way according to their custom). They do not eat shellfish or drink alcohol.
- Hindus do not eat beef (they believe the cow is a sacred animal). Many are vegan, but some do eat lamb, poultry and/or fish.
- Some Sikhs eat all types of meat or fish. Others avoid meat and/or fish.
- Jews do not eat pork, bacon or ham, shellfish or eels. They do not eat meat or milk at the same time or cooked together (e.g. lasagne). They eat kosher meat (i.e. meat that has been prepared in accordance with Jewish dietary guidelines). Milk and milk products are usually eaten at breakfast only and avoided at other meals.
- Rastafarians do not eat processed foods (any food produced in a factory), pork or eels, or drink alcohol, tea or coffee.

Medical diets

There are many medical reasons why people cannot eat certain foods. They include diseases such as diabetes, allergies such as nut allergy and food intolerances such as gluten or lactose intolerance. With rising levels of people with obesity, high blood pressure and heart attacks, many people are advised to cut their fat, calorie, sugar and/or salt intake.

Some of these diets are outlined below:

- People with diabetes find it difficult to control their blood sugar levels, so need to eat starchy foods at regular intervals. They should avoid dishes that are high in sugar.

Sugar-free chocolates for people with diabetes

- People who are on a low-fat diet should avoid foods that are naturally high in fat, e.g. cheese, bacon, butter, margarine, spreads and foods that are fried or roasted in fat.
- People who are on a low-salt diet should avoid most processed foods, smoked meats, cheese and Chinese foods containing monosodium glutamate.
- People who have a nut allergy must avoid nuts, blended cooking oils and margarines that contain nut oils. They must read food labels carefully – most state that foods 'may contain nuts' or have been 'prepared in an area that may contain nuts'.
- People who have lactose intolerance must avoid milk, cheese, butter, yogurt and processed foods that contain milk products. They must read food labels carefully.
- People who have a gluten intolerance (or coeliac disease) must avoid wheat, wholemeal, whole wheat and wheat meal flour, bran, pasta, noodles, semolina, bread, pastry, sauces thickened with flour, muesli, wheat, rye, barley and oat breakfast cereals, beer, and other malted drinks. However, they can eat rice, potatoes, corn and corn products. They must read food labels carefully.

 WARNING

This product may contain nuts

 ACTIVITY

How would you choose suitable dishes from this menu if you:

- are a vegetarian?
- suffer from diabetes?
- have a nut allergy?

ℳain courses

Steak and chips £6.99
Prime Scottish steak and our famous chunky chips.
Cooked how you like it and served with your choice of pepper,
mushroom or blue cheese sauce.

Grilled salmon £5.99
A fillet of wild salmon seasoned with cajun spices and grilled.
Served with new potatoes and seasonal vegetables.

[V] **Tomato and basil pasta** £5.50
Fresh penne pasta in a rich tomato and basil sauce.
Served with garlic bread.

Chicken tikka masala £5.99
A medium-hot curry made from an authentic recipe.
Served on basmati rice and accompanied with poppadoms
and mango chutney.

[V] **Spinach and goat's cheese bake** £5.99
A burst of flavour from fresh spinach and goat's cheese.
wrapped in filo pastry and served with salad.

 TERMINOLOGY:

Allergy: an adverse reaction by the body to certain substances (including foods).

Food intolerance: condition obliging someone to avoid a certain food because of the effect on their body.

Allgeric reaction: the way in which the body responds to some foods, for example: a rash, swelling and anaphylactic shock.

Other health issues

Obesity

During the early twenty-first century, the number of people with obesity has risen sharply. What is particularly worrying is the increasing number of children who are suffering from obesity. It is estimated that by 2010 three in every five adults will be obese and two in every five children will be obese. In the UK alone, over 30,000 premature deaths a year are linked to obesity. The cost to the country for medical treatment, time off work and care is estimated at over £7.5 billion a year. These are frightening statistics!

What is obesity?

People with a body mass index (BMI) of more than 30 are termed obese. Body mass index can be calculated by knowing your height (in metres) and your weight (in kilograms).

BMI = weight divided by height squared (height × height)

ADULT BMI CHART

Under 20	underweight
20–25	normal
25–30	overweight
30–35	obese
Over 35	morbidly obese (i.e. life is at risk)

ACTIVITY

1. Work out the BMI for a person who is 1.5 metres tall and weighs 50 kg.

2. Work out the BMI for a person who is 1.6 metres tall and weighs 80 kg.

   Here is the answer to question 1:

   50 divided by (1.5 × 1.5)

   50 divided by 2.25 = 22

3. Look at the chart below. What does the BMI of the second person indicate?

What causes obesity?

The energy we get from food is measured in calories. Obesity is caused by eating more food, i.e. having a higher calorie intake, than is needed by the body. Fat is the body's energy reservoir. The body needs normal levels of fat to function properly. Fat is stored under the skin, but there is also some fat around the kidneys and inside the liver and muscles. Other parts of the body where fat collects depends on whether you are a man or a woman. Men tend to have fat on the chest, waist and buttocks. Women tend to have fat on the breasts, waist, hips and buttocks.

Fat tissue is made up of fat cells. The cells are like tiny plastic bags that hold drops of fat. Fat cells are formed in childhood. If fat is stored quickly, more fat cells are created. A fat child can have up to three times as many fat cells as a normal child. Fat cells stop multiplying in adulthood so an adult has a fixed number of cells for life. A fat child is much more likely to become a fat adult.

What medical problems are associated with obesity?

In children, medical problems of obesity are not always obvious. Sometimes the soft tissue in the back of the throat blocks the airways, causing them to stop breathing for up to a minute. This can happen several times a night, leading to heart problems, headaches, memory loss and tiredness. In adults, being obese increases the risks of many diseases and health problems, including:

- high levels of cholesterol
- coronary heart disease
- gall bladder problems
- strokes
- osteoarthritis
- respiratory (breathing) problems and shortness of breath
- some cancers (e.g. breast and colon)
- Type 2 diabetes
- stress.

What is the treatment for obesity?

There are several treatments for obesity, some more drastic than others. The most obvious way of treating obesity is by changing eating habits and lifestyle. Unfortunately, very few obese people are able to keep their weight down. There are several weight loss drugs available – these work either by lowering hunger levels (an appetite suppressant) or by increasing metabolic rate (the rate at which people burn calories).

Some people have surgical procedures (operations) to clamp or staple their stomachs so that they are able to limit the type and amount of food they eat. Others have liposuction to draw off excess fat. All operations carry risks.

Before starting to plan any menu, there are four basic questions that you should ask:

1. Who is going to eat the meal? Consider age, gender, occupation, specific dietary needs, etc.
2. When is it going to be eaten? Consider time of year, time of day, etc.
3. Where is it going to be eaten? Consider venue, space available, cooking or re-heating facilities available, etc.
4. What is going to be eaten? Consider time of day, type of menu requested, e.g. sit down meal or buffet, special occasions, etc.

When these basic questions have been answered, there are many other factors to consider in planning a well-balanced menu. We look at the most important factor first – the nutritional needs of the customer.

Nutritional needs

Good health relies on good nutritious food. Nutritional needs must be considered carefully in residential establishments (such as care homes, hospitals, prisons, schools) where people have little choice about what they eat.

Everyone needs the following:

- protein – for growth and repair of body cells
- carbohydrates (starches and sugars) for energy and physical activity
- fats – for body warmth, energy and protection of body organs (e.g. the kidneys)
- vitamins and minerals – for protection against disease and to regulate body functions
- water – for body processes like digestion and for controlling body temperature
- fibre – for the healthy working of the digestive system.

The amount of each nutrient needed depends on a person's age, gender, occupation and lifestyle.

Young children

Young children need protein for growth and development. Children should be given small, attractive portions of food. They should be introduced to new foods gradually. Fatty foods and sugary foods and drinks should be avoided.

Teenagers

Teenagers also need a good supply of protein. Worries about being overweight and poor skin are typical of this age group. Eating five portions a day of fruit and vegetables will encourage healthy skin. Fruit and vegetables are high in vitamins and fibre and contain virtually no fat, so can help maintain a healthy weight. A good supply of iron is needed, especially for teenage girls when they start menstruation (periods). Again, fatty foods and sugary foods and drinks should be avoided. Careful and sensible eating is essential to lay down good habits for adulthood.

Pensioners

Pensioners need protein to repair worn out body cells. They need a good supply of calcium and Vitamin D in order to maintain healthy bones and teeth and iron to keep blood healthy. In winter time, they may need a little more fat in their diet to provide body warmth. Fresh fruit and vegetables are important for a good supply of vitamins and minerals. Old people may have digestive problems (an inability to digest certain foods) or may have difficulty cutting food (because of arthritis) or chewing food (because of false teeth).

Special diets

This aspect applies particularly to caterers who are planning meals for patients in hospitals or homes. In a hospital, dieticians will ensure the correct foods are given in the correct quantity. Generally foods rich in Vitamin C are given to help the healing process. Foods high in starch, sugar and fat are reduced so that patients do not put on too much weight. Foods are served in small, colourful portions to encourage eating if there is loss of appetite.

Other factors

Next, we look at other factors that you need to take into account when planning menus that are suitable for customers.

Vegetarian dishes

Vegetarian dishes are popular, especially when there are concerns about diseases and outbreaks of food poisoning linked to meat (salmonella, E-Coli, BSE ('mad cow' disease), 'bird flu', etc.) Vegetable dishes and salads help to satisfy customers and offer variety in terms of colour, texture and taste. They also make the menu cheaper to produce. See also page 00.

Religious and ethnic diets

People of some faiths do not eat meat. As a general rule, Jews and Muslims do not eat pork and Hindus do not eat beef. Most religious diets are catered for with either vegan or vegetarian dishes. By law, every restaurant must offer at least one dish that is suitable for vegetarians. In practice, most restaurants offer more than this, in order to attract customers. There are many 'ethnic' restaurants in the UK, each serving a mix of traditional and 'anglicised' dishes (for example, Indian, Chinese and Thai dishes are all very popular).

Time of year and weather

Generally, we prefer hot food in cold weather and cold food in hot weather. In winter, dishes such as stews, casseroles and roasts are in demand. In summer, salads and foods like fish and chicken in light sauces are preferred. Caterers often make use of foods 'in season' when they are cheap and good quality to create popular seasonal menus. Traditionally, special dishes are served at certain times of the year, for example roast turkey or goose at Christmas, pancakes on Shrove Tuesday, Spring lamb at Easter. Muslims traditionally eat roast lamb at Tobaski or Eid.

Type of customer

Customers choose where and what to eat because of many different reasons. They may want a celebration meal, a snack while they are out shopping, a lunch to socialise with friends, a meal during a business meeting or a buffet party to celebrate a christening, wedding or birthday. Customers will have different needs at different times.

Time available

As a general rule, the shorter the time available to cook, serve and eat the food, the more limited (smaller) the menu. Fast-food outlets offer a limited menu, where all items can be cooked quickly. Customers queue and collect their own food, pay before they eat, and find their own tables or take food away. If they eat on site, they are encouraged to clear their own tables at the end.

Restaurants such as Harvester and Beefeater offer customers a more relaxed 'meal experience'. Customers wait to be seated and they order drinks and meals from serving staff. They collect their own salads from the salad cart, but meals and drinks are served to them. The tables are cleared and the bill is taken to the customer after they have eaten. Generally, self service is much faster than waiter/waitress service.

Price of menu

Customers are generally willing to pay a fair price for a fair portion. The price the caterer can charge will depend on the quality of the food and the surroundings. The price you would expect to pay for a meal in McDonald's would not be the same as you would expect to pay in a five-star hotel, where you are paying not only for the food but the service and the surroundings.

STARTERS	
Tomato and basil soup	£3.75
Melon and Parma ham	£3.75
Breaded prawns with sweet chilli dipping sauce	£4.99
Garlic bread	£3.50

Caterers working in residential establishments like hospitals, homes, prisons and schools usually have only a limited budget, so have to keep costs to a minimum.

Commercial establishments have to make a profit in order to stay in business. The selling price (price shown on the menu) must consider:

- food costs
- overheads (gas, electricity, lighting, rates and rent)
- labour costs (staff wages)
- profit.

The actual food costs are calculated at about 40 per cent of the selling price. This means that if a dish costs £4 per portion to make, it would be sold for £10 per portion.

Portion control

Apple crumble made in individual portions

Portion control concerns the amount of each menu item produced and served. It will depend upon the type of customer, the actual food item (some foods are very rich and only served in small portions) and the selling price of the food.

Good portion control is needed to:

- keep costs down
- keep losses in food preparation and serving to a minimum
- to offer customers a 'satisfying' portion without waste
- to make a profit.

Portions can be 'marked' in the kitchen, i.e. cutting lines are marked on dishes to show how big the portions should be. Careful garnishes or decorations (e.g. on a gateau or cheesecake) will also indicate portion size. There is also a range of equipment that can be used to portion food:

- scoops – used for ice cream, mashed potatoes
- ladles – used for soups, sauces and gravies
- fruit juice glasses – for fruit juice
- individual pie dishes – shepherds pie, fish pie, steak and onion pie, steak and kidney pie, lasagne
- ramekins – egg custards, mousses, pâtés
- sundae dishes – fruit salads
- individual moulds – jellies, mousses
- individual pudding basins – summer pudding, Christmas pudding, steamed pudding, sticky toffee pudding
- coupés – ice cream
- butter-pat machines – butter
- milk dispensers – milk
- soup plates or bowls
- serving spoons/tablespoons – fruit or vegetables.

Ability of chef/cook

The ability of the cook has a great influence on the menu offered. If staff are not highly trained it would be better to offer a simple menu that can be beautifully cooked and served. Many establishments rely on cook-chill or cook-freeze dishes. These need 'regeneration' (heating to required temperature) only and therefore do not need skilled staff. The more convenience foods used, the lower the level of skill needed.

A combi oven

Equipment available

The amount of equipment will depend on how complicated the menu is, the type of food to be cooked and the number of meals to be served. Some foods (for example cook-chill foods) only need regeneration so there is no need for a full range of kitchen equipment. If fresh foods are used a full range of preparation and cooking equipment is needed.

An industrial steamer

Methods of cooking

A menu will be more attractive to customers if food is cooked in a variety of ways (e.g. boiled, baked, fried, grilled, poached, roasted, stewed). In a small or busy kitchen it is important to consider the cooking methods carefully, otherwise some pieces of equipment will be in constant use and cause delays, while other pieces of equipment may not be used at all. For example, if a lot of fried food is on offer, the friture (deep-fat fryer) may be over-used. Also, too much fried food on a menu will not offer customers a healthier option.

Here are two examples of poor menu planning:

- fried fish and chips followed by apple fritters (all fried)
- Irish stew, boiled potatoes and peas followed by stewed rhubarb and custard (all cooked in liquid).

A deep fat fryer

Ability of serving staff

Many high-class establishments (e.g. five-star hotels) used to have highly trained wait staff who were able to provide silver service, i.e. transfer food from a serving dish to the customers plate with great skill. Nowadays, the majority of high-class establishments use 'plated service' where the food is styled in the kitchen by the chef and served directly to the customer. The ability to look after customers and provide good customer care is considered to be more important than service skills.

Balance

To achieve a good balance, choose courses that vary from light to heavy. That way, customers will not feel bloated, nor will they think that they have not had their money's worth.

Balance means considering all of the following things.

Variety of ingredients

Try not to repeat ingredients from one course to another, e.g. tomato soup followed by mixed grill served with chipped potatoes, tomatoes and peas.

Colour

Add colourful vegetables, salads, garnishes or decorations if possible to 'lift' the colour of food on the plate. Remember that white, cream, green and brown are 'dead' colours and too much of one of these colours will make food look boring and flat.

Flavour

Do not repeat strong flavours from one course to another, e.g. garlic mushrooms followed by lasagne and garlic bread. Use strong-flavoured foods and herbs with care. Try not to over-season food so that customers cannot taste the natural flavours.

Texture

Contrasting textures are important to give variety and interest to a meal, e.g. croutons with soup, wafers with ice-cream. Try to include foods that are soft and foods that need to be chewed, bitten or crunched. Remember that cooking changes the texture of food, so cooking times are important when cooking foods like rice, pasta, vegetables and steaks.

Shape

This is particularly important when serving buffet food. Try to include as many shapes as possible to provide interest, e.g. sausage rolls, chicken twizzles, tuna baskets, mini-quiches, cream-cheese stars, stuffed cherry tomatoes, cheese and kiwi or cheese and grapes on sticks, cream horns, meringues, etc. Chefs often 'stack' food attractively on plates to add shape where there is none. Shaped plates can also add interest to plain food.

Presentation

One of the aims of a chef is to make food look (and taste) as appetising as possible. When thinking about presentation, you need to consider:

- consistency (how thin or how thick)
- texture (e.g. crunchy, soft, crisp)
- flavour (e.g. salty, sweet, sour, bitter, well-seasoned)
- seasoning (e.g. use of salt, pepper, herbs and spices)
- colour
- accompaniments (e.g. colourful vegetables and sauces)
- decoration (used on sweet dishes, e.g. chocolate leaves, fresh fruit)
- garnish (used on savoury dishes, e.g. parsley, tomatoes).

Do not over-season, over-decorate or over-fill dishes. The golden rule for all food presentation is keep it clean, neat, simple and colourful.

Garnishes should not be 'sprinkled' over dishes – the substance is difficult to remove if the customer does not like it.

Food that needs to be served hot should be hot (and not warm) and served on hot plates. Food that needs to be served cold should be served cold (but not frozen) and always on cold plates. Food probes can be used to check the temperature of food.

Savoury food is usually served in oval dishes or on oval plates with a dish paper if needed. Sweet food is usually served in round dishes or on round plates with a sweet paper if needed.

Planning a range of menus

What types of menu are available?

- Table d'hôte or set-price menu – a 'fixed' or set-price menu usually consists of two or three courses with a limited selection of dishes available at every course.
- À la carte menu – a menu where all the dishes are individually priced and cooked to order.
- Party or function menu – this type of menu can vary from drinks and canapés to a sit-down banquet for an event (e.g. wedding, anniversary, dinner dance, conference, meeting, corporate event). This type of menu usually has a fixed price and is often chosen beforehand (so that guests are not given a choice).
- Ethnic or speciality menu – this can be fixed price or à la carte. Speciality food of a particular country may be on offer (e.g. Chinese or Mexican) or the food itself could be specialised (e.g. fish, pasta, ice-cream, pancakes, pies, vegetarian).
- Fast-food menu – this is similar in some ways to a speciality menu. It may have a theme like burgers, baked potatoes or fried chicken. All items are priced separately and 'finished' or cooked on demand.
- Rotating menu cycle – this is a 'fixed pattern' of menus that covers a 'fixed number' of days (called the menu cycle). The fixed number of days always includes a number of weeks plus 1 day (i.e. 8 days, 15 days, 22 days, etc.). The addition of the extra day means that menu items are not repeated on the same day each week.

Other types of menu cater for people at work, patients in hospitals, school children and people who are travelling (e.g. on planes, trains, ferries, cruise ships)

ACTIVITY

Try to find examples of each type of menu. Local newspapers often have adverts for restaurants that offer table d'hôte, à la carte and party menus. Look out for take-away menus (e.g. Chinese, Indian or pizza). Find out if your local primary school offers a rotating menu.

Portion control

Portion control concerns the amount of each menu item produced and served. It will depend upon the type of customer, the actual food item (some foods are very rich and only served in small portions) and the selling price of the food.

Good portion control is needed to:

- keep costs down
- keep losses in food preparation and serving to a minimum
- to offer customers a 'satisfying' portion without waste
- to make a profit.

Portions can be 'marked' in the kitchen, i.e. cutting lines are marked on dishes to show how big the portions should be. Careful garnishes or decorations (e.g. on a gateau or cheesecake) will also indicate portion size. There is also a range of equipment that can be used to portion food:

- scoops – used for ice cream, mashed potatoes
- ladles – used for soups, sauces and gravies
- fruit juice glasses – for fruit juice
- individual pie dishes – shepherds pie, fish pie, steak and onion pie, steak and kidney pie, lasagne
- ramekins – egg custards, mousses, pâtés
- sundae dishes – fruit salads
- individual moulds – jellies, mousses
- individual pudding basins – summer pudding, Christmas pudding, steamed pudding, sticky toffee pudding
- coupés – ice cream
- butter-pat machines – butter
- milk dispensers – milk
- soup plates or bowls
- serving spoons/tablespoons – fruit or vegetables.

As a guide, you can generally allow the following:

- soup 4–6 portions per litre
- meat 6–8 portions per kg

- cold meat 16 portions per kg
- potatoes 8 portions per kg
- vegetables 6–8 portions per kg
- sauces 8–12 portions per ½ kg.

Portion control is extremely important. Customers need to feel they are getting 'value for money' and having the same size portion as everyone else. It helps the caterer when **planning** (how many portions will these ingredients make?) considering **selling price** (how much should I charge to cover costs and make a profit?) and avoids waste.

Using standard recipes can help a caterer by determining how many ingredients will make 10, 20, 30 or more portions. Using dishes of a standard size will also help.

The next two activities use a straightforward recipe (a strawberry gateau made by the whisking method) to help you understand about portion control and costing.

ACTIVITY

On a piece of A4 size paper, draw the outline of the sandwich tin used to bake the strawberry gateau. Show a 'bird's eye' view of how it will be decorated. Label the diagram.

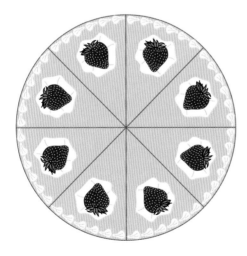

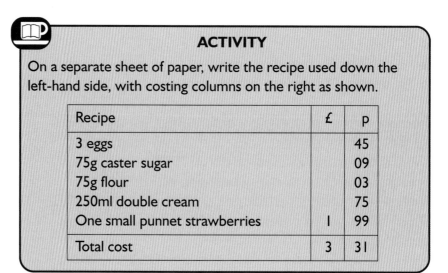

ACTIVITY

On a separate sheet of paper, write the recipe used down the left-hand side, with costing columns on the right as shown.

Recipe	£	p
3 eggs		45
75g caster sugar		09
75g flour		03
250ml double cream		75
One small punnet strawberries	1	99
Total cost	3	31

Once you have the total price of the gateau, you need to calculate the price per portion:

- The gateau made 8 portions, therefore the price of 1 portion is the total price ÷ 8.
- The gateau cost £3.31 for 8 portions, therefore 1 portion costs £3.31 ÷ 8.
- This works out at 42 pence per portion (to the nearest penny).

This section is all about the safe use of equipment in the industry. You should be able to identify a range of specialist equipment and explain how to use them safely and hygienically. This includes the following.

Small and large-scale catering equipment:

- hand equipment
- powered equipment
- food storage equipment.

Small and large-scale food service equipment:

- hand equipment
- powered equipment.

Catering equipment

Hand equipment

Small items of equipment include cooking tins, knives, kitchen utensils such as ladles, spoons, whisks and spatulas and small items of cookery equipment such as frying pans and saucepans.

Use and care of small equipment:

- Small pieces of equipment are expensive and are easily lost or damaged.
- All small equipment should be washed immediately after use, rinsed, dried and replaced in a clean storage area or rack.
- Ensure that small items, e.g. potato peelers, are not thrown away with rubbish.
- Never put knives in a washing up sink or bowl as they may cause injury to staff.
- Keep knives sharp and stored safely.

Powered equipment

Powered equipment includes small items such as electric mixers, microwaves, food processors and blenders,

medium-sized equipment such as mincing machines, potato chippers and floor-standing mixers, and large-scale equipment such as ovens, fryers, hot plates, steamers, bratt pans and grills. Computer-controlled cooking equipment is widely used in the industry.

Use and care of powered equipment:

- The manufacturer's instructions should be followed at all times when using and cleaning powered equipment.
- A qualified electrician should service electrical equipment regularly.
- Only trained staff should use certain items of equipment.
- Safety notices should be placed on all equipment.
- All equipment should be switched off when not in use.
- Position small powered equipment carefully so there is no danger when in use.

Food storage equipment

There must be very high standards of hygiene in any area used for food storage. Good lighting and ventilation are essential in dry-stores. The quality and safety of chilled and frozen foods depend upon them being stored at the correct temperature. Food storage equipment such as freezers, blast chillers, chilled cabinets and refrigerators are therefore vitally important.

Use and care of food storage equipment:

- Refrigerators, freezers and chilled cabinets must be cleaned (and defrosted) regularly.
- Never put hot food into refrigerators or freezers – it will raise the temperature to an unsafe level.
- Monitor and record temperatures at least twice a day.
- Keep food covered.
- Service regularly.
- Store all cleaning materials away from food storage areas.

Food service equipment

Hand equipment

This includes the crockery, cutlery, table linen and glassware used to lay tables, as well as serving equipment and the tables, chairs and sideboards found in food service areas.

The type of crockery, cutlery, table linen and glassware used will depend upon the type of menu and service offered, the cost, and the washing-up facilities. Many fast-food restaurants use disposable items such as plastic cutlery and polystyrene cups and have easy-to-clean tables. High-class restaurants, on the other hand, may use fine porcelain crockery, linen tablecloths and napkins, crystal glasses and silver cutlery.

Use and care of hand equipment:

- Choose cutlery carefully – plain cutlery is easier to clean than patterned cutlery and stainless steel cutlery resists scratches.
- Cutlery should be stored carefully to avoid scratches and marks.
- Glassware should be washed, stored and handled carefully to avoid breakages.
- Crockery should be dishwasher proof.
- Crockery should be stacked carefully and covered if possible to prevent dust and germs settling.
- Use slips where possible over linen cloths to cut down cleaning costs.
- Store linen, same sizes together in a cupboard away from dust.

Powered equipment

A wide range of powered equipment is used in food service areas. This includes hand-held credit or debit card payment facilities, coffee machines, toasters, vending machines, flambé trolleys and hot and cold service counters. EPOS (electronic point of sale) can be used to send orders from the restaurant and bar to the kitchen and reception – this assists staff with the customers' bills.

Use and care of powered equipment:

- All electrical equipment must be checked for safety every year.
- All equipment on view in a food service area should be spotlessly clean and polished daily.
- Flambé trolleys should not be moved around a restaurant with food or equipment on it.
- Spirits, e.g. brandy, should be handled carefully when flaming dishes.

- The temperature of hot and cold food service areas should be monitored and recorded daily.
- Coffee machines should be kept clean at all times and serviced regularly.

ACTIVITY

1. Find out how EPOS works.
2. Identify three pieces of industrial machinery used in catering kitchens.
3. Find out how often food storage temperatures are taken.
4. What temperature should food be stored at in a freezer, a refrigerator and a dry store?

What types of communication and record-keeping are necessary in the hospitality and catering industry?

Let's look at the types of communication used and what they are used for.

Types of communication	Use
Verbal	Giving instructions to others, talking to clients, taking messages.
Written	Confirmation of bookings, memos, promotions, letters, taking orders for food and drink.
Telephone	Taking messages, giving responses.
Fax	Information, ordering, newsletters, internal memos.
ICT	Staff rotas, bookings, accounts, invoices, room management, booking events and functions, orders, stock control.

It is important that **record-keeping** is accurate and appropriate. This enables staff to check on a booking or an order, without the need for the member of staff who took the booking or placed the order to be there.

Communication is important across all areas of the industry. Each department has to know what is happening. For example, if the reception did not tell the chef or head waiter how many people had booked in, they would not know how many to cater for or to set covers for. Or if the chef did not tell the wait staff what foods were available, the wait staff could not tell the customers, who may then order something that is not on the menu.

Staff have to communicate effectively with each other to ensure things get done quickly. They also have to communicate well with customers. It is important that customers feel they can approach the staff if they require assistance or if there is a problem.

To communicate well, staff should:

- be friendly
- be smart
- be clean
- have good verbal communication skills
- have good written skills
- be able to use ICT effectively.

Communicating by telephone

A telephone call is often the first contact that the customer has with the industry. If a call is not handled correctly it could lead to the loss of a customer. First impressions count and have a big impact on the customer. Staff who answer telephone calls should be trained in how to get the correct information from the customer and how to:

- transfer calls
- place callers on hold
- arrange conference calls
- sell products and services
- page other staff
- connect calls, both internally and externally
- make calls.

The communication equipment that staff may use include:

- single and multiple line telephones
- email and the internet
- answering machines
- fax machines
- mobile phones
- pagers
- switchboard and extensions.

It is important that staff who answer the telephone know how to respond confidently and effectively. It is important to leave a good impression with the customer. The answering procedure should be the same for everyone answering a call in order to maintain consistency. It is also important to be discreet; information about guests should not be discussed with other staff, unless absolutely necessary. Messages in any format should only be given to the person they are intended for.

When answering a call, staff should follow this basic procedure:

- Answer the call promptly – ideally a caller should wait no more than between three and six rings.
- Pick up the telephone with a smile (it relaxes the muscles in the face so that the voice is friendly).
- Start with a polite greeting, e.g. 'Good Morning'.
- Identify the establishment, e.g. 'The Royal Hotel'.
- Identify yourself, e.g. 'This is Judy'.
- Ask how you can be of assistance, e.g. 'How may I help you?'

This way, the customer knows immediately that they have phoned the correct number, and who they are speaking to.

Customers phone an establishment for a number of reasons. They may phone to:

- make a booking
- find out about the facilities that are available
- make a complaint
- make general enquiries
- report a security risk
- arrange an appointment
- request room service
- arrange delivery of goods.

Telephone manners

It is important to be polite when answering the phone. We should remember to:

- speak clearly
- be courteous
- establish the reason for the call
- pay attention to what the caller is saying
- transfer the call to the appropriate department
- pass messages on promptly
- be professional at all times.

If the customer does not give all the information we need, we can find out the reason for the call by asking questions. There are three different types of question we can ask:

- open questions – to obtain information. These type of questions usually begin with 'why', 'how', 'when' and 'what'.

- closed questions – these are used to ensure that you obtain the correct facts, e.g. 'How many would you like, sir?'
- reflective questions – these are used to ensure you have got all the correct information. You may repeat the information the customer has given you to check it is correct, e.g. 'So, that is a table for four, at seven o'clock this evening?'

Good customer service is important. You can help to achieve it by:

- having a good knowledge of the products and services your establishment offers
- having a good knowledge of personnel (other staff who work in the establishment) and their job roles, to enable you to pass the information to the correct person
- relaying messages promptly
- handling calls efficiently and courteously.

ACTIVITY

With a partner, take turns to roleplay scenarios of phone calls in the catering industry, for example:

- a booking for a restaurant
- a customer complaining about the service they have received
- a delivery driver requesting directions.

Within the catering industry it is important that we take into account environmental issues. You should have an understanding of how to conserve energy and water when preparing food, how to reduce, reuse and recycle waste in the preparation and serving of meals, and why it is important for the industry to address these areas.

Conservation of energy and water

There are many ways in which the catering industry can conserve energy and water and ask customers to do the same:

- Turn equipment and lights off when not in use
- Invest in energy-efficient equipment, especially refrigerators, freezers, washing machines and cookers
- Keep equipment as clean as possible – uses less energy
- Never put hot food into refrigerators – it raises the temperature to an unsafe level and makes the motor work too hard, thus wasting energy
- Have regular maintenance checks
- Put lids on pans when boiling water
- Have efficient temperature control (heating and ventilation)
- Have full loads for washing machines and dishwashers
- Have energy efficient lights in dining areas
- Install modern toilets that use less flush water in staff and customer cloakrooms
- Only serve water on tables when customers request it.

Reduce, reuse, recycle

Catering establishments can reduce, reuse and recycle the waste they produce by:

- Buying ingredients that are fresh or in less packaging
- Buying ingredients in bulk
- Sending food waste to local farms for animal feed
- Putting vegetable peelings onto a compost heap for the garden; many hotels grow their own fruit, vegetables and herbs

Reduce

Recycle   Reuse

- Recycling all plastic, glass, paper and card
- Reusing large containers for storing goods
- Encouraging customers to recycle by putting recycle bins around the establishment
- Using bio-degradable products that are less harmful to the environment.

It is important for the catering industry to act responsibly and encourage customers to consider the environment as it not only gives the industry a good reputation but also allows customers to see that establishments care about what is happening in the world. Setting a good example encourages others to do the same.

REMEMBER

Remember the 3 Rs: Reduce, Reuse, Recycle.

Advances in technology mean that foods can be packaged in such a way that they can be kept for longer periods of time.

Why do we package food?

Food needs suitable packaging to:

- protect the contents
- hold the contents
- keep food fresh
- reduce food waste
- make food easier to handle, transport and serve
- improve hygiene
- make the contents look more attractive
- give information on contents, storage and use.

Types of packaging

Packaging	Advantages	Disadvantages
Paper and card	Easily printed Can be recycled Strong when dry Lightweight	Crushes easily Weak when wet Recycled paper and card cannot be used for food
Glass	Easily printed Strong Reusable Recyclable Can carry liquids	Brittle (easily broken)
MAP (modified atmosphere packaging)	Enables foods like fresh meat, fresh fish and salads to have a longer 'shelf life'	Once packaging is opened food will deteriorate quickly
Metal	Recyclable Easily printed Strong Rigid	Must be coated inside or reacts with food Cannot microwave Uses valuable energy to extract from ground
Plastic and polystyrene	Strong Flexible Easily printed Does not react with food	Causes litter problem Limited resource Not easily recycled

Food packaging used in catering

Takeaway food establishments in particular use a lot of packaging. Some examples are given below.

Cardboard boxes are used for pizzas because they:

- are easy to print
- 'soak up' excess grease
- keep pizza hot
- protect the pizza from damage when carrying
- are easy to assemble and stack.

Polystyrene boxes are used for burgers, fish and chips, etc. because they:

- are strong
- are easy to print
- are light to carry
- do not react with food
- act as an insulator to keep food hot.

Clear plastic sandwich boxes are used for sandwiches because they:

- are light to carry
- allow the customers to see the contents easily
- keep the sandwiches fresh
- keep the sandwiches hygienic.

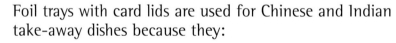

Foil trays with card lids are used for Chinese and Indian take-away dishes because they:

- keep the food hot
- can be written on (the lids) to identify the contents
- can stack easily
- are lightweight.

Plastic containers with lids are used for Chinese and Indian take-away dishes because they:

- keep the food hot
- seal tightly to prevent leakage
- can be used in a microwave
- can be washed and reused
- do not react with food.

Food manufacturers are trying to reduce the amount of packaging used for food products. Customers are encouraged to reuse and recycle food packaging whenever possible.

CHAPTER 2

ASSESSMENT FOR GCSE CATERING (SINGLE AWARD)

2.1 CONTROLLED ASSESSMENTS

Unit 1 is assessed through **two** practical tasks, externally set by the examination board. The two tasks are worth 60 per cent of the final grade for the Single Award in Catering.

If you are studying for the Double Award in Hospitality and Catering you should note that the two tasks are worth 30 per cent of the final grade.

Task 1 – 20 per cent
To be selected from a bank of three set tasks. This will be internally marked and externally moderated. Task 1 should take up to 15 hours.

Task 2 – 40 per cent
To be selected from a bank of three set tasks. This will be internally marked and externally moderated. Task 2 should take up to 30 hours.

Task 1 is based on commodities that are widely used in the catering industry. You will need to complete a practical assessment based on fruit and vegetables, rice and pasta or dairy products.

Task 2 is based on meal preparation and you will need to be able to dovetail tasks effectively. The meals are based on international cookery, healthy eating or vegetarian cookery.

Task 1 will be marked as follows:

- Planning the task (10 marks)
- Carrying out the task (20 marks)
- Evaluating the task (10 marks).

Planning the task (10 marks)

In order to gain high marks in this section you need to show that you have investigated the chosen commodities so that you can make an informed choice of dishes to prepare for the practical.

The following points should help to guide you when carrying out your research:

- Ease of obtaining
- Cost
- Storage
- Uses
- Types/varieties available
- Versatility
- Ease of preparation and cooking
- Colour, flavour and texture
- Nutritive value.

You can carry out your research in a number of ways:

- Produce a display
- Organise tasting sessions
- Try out new recipes
- Visit local shops, markets and restaurants
- Have talks or demonstrations from visiting speakers.

Note: There is a limit of four pages or eight sides for the planning and evaluation sections of Task 1.

A healthy dish: salmon with spring vegetables

You must choose a **selection of dishes** that will reflect not only the commodities but also your **skill** as a cook. Remember to use the checklist in the section on 'Food preparation skills' so that you have included some high-level skills in your chosen dishes.

A good way of doing this is to list the dishes you have chosen and state what skills and methods of cookery are being shown, for example:

- macaroni cheese: sauce making, cooking pasta, boiling, grilling (once coated in cheese and breadcrumbs)
- strawberry gateau: whisking method, decorating skills, baking.

On paper, draw how you expect your final dishes to look. In this way you can assess the range of colours, shapes and textures you will use.

Your teachers should act as a guide and prompt at this stage – asking questions and giving suggestions for improvement before you make your final choices.

Prepare a written plan to show:

- the dishes you have chosen, with reasons for your choice
- the time plan and/or order of work
- the shopping list.

Carrying out the task (20 marks)

In order to gain high marks in this section you need to demonstrate:

- high standards of personal hygiene (e.g. wearing of apron/whites, hair back, no nail varnish, no jewellery)
- good personal hygiene habits (e.g. no licking fingers, tasting with a clean teaspoon)
- safe use of equipment, especially knives, pans and electrical equipment
- selection of the correct tools (e.g. correct knife for chopping, peeling)
- use of a wide variety of commodities within the task chosen (e.g. not all cheese dishes for dairy products)
- good food hygiene (e.g. perishable foods refrigerated, not left on work unit/table, using temperature probes to ensure food is cooked)
- neat, organised work

- safe use of oven and hob
- working to time
- independent working
- good technical skills
- little food waste
- logical sequence of work, e.g. food that needs to be cooked for a long time, be set or served cold needs to be made first
- a wide variety of skills
- high standard of final presentation, e.g. portion control, use of garnish and decoration, good colour, correct temperature, correct texture, good flavour, appropriate serving dishes.

Evaluating the task (10 marks)

In order to gain high marks in this section you need to discuss:

- the suitability of dishes chosen. Did your dishes reflect the use of the commodity in the industry? If they did, why? If not, why not?
- any changes you would make to the choice of dishes and why
- time management
- how customers (consumers) would regard your dishes in terms of appearance, flavour and texture
- what improvements you would make and why
- the size and cost per portion (see costing instructions in section on evaluating the task and calculating selling price).

Task 2 will be marked as follows:

- Investigating and planning the task (25 marks)
- Carrying out the task (40 marks)
- Evaluating the task (15 marks).

Investigating and planning the task (25 marks)

You need to investigate food from other countries and cultures, the government guidelines on healthy eating in schools, or vegetarianism.

Beware of presenting work taken directly from the internet. If you are going to carry out research on the internet, then you must identify the work clearly and acknowledge where it came from. You should comment on all research *in your own words*. In order to gain high marks for this section you will need to show that you have included information from a wide range of resources.

You can carry out your research in a number of ways. You could:

- Produce a display
- Organise tasting sessions
- Try out new recipes
- Organise visits to local restaurants offering vegetarian and ethnic dishes
- Have talks or demonstrations from visiting speakers.

Note: There is a limit of 10 pages or 20 sides for the research, planning and evaluation of Task 2.

You must choose a two-course meal that will reflect your skill as a cook.

Remember to use the checklist in the 'Food preparation skills' section so that you have included several high level skills in your chosen dishes. On paper, draw how you expect your final dishes to look; in this way you can assess the range of colours, shapes and textures you have chosen.

You should avoid using dishes that show too much cream, brown or green – they are known as 'dead' colours and too much of one colour will make your food look dull and uninteresting.

Your teachers should act as a guide and prompt at this stage – asking questions and giving suggestions for improvement before you make your final choices.

Prepare a written plan to show:

- the dishes you have chosen, with reasons for your choice
- the time plan and/or order of work
- the shopping list.

Carrying out the task (40 marks)

In order to gain high marks in this section you need to demonstrate:

- high standards of personal hygiene (e.g. wearing of apron/whites, hair back, no nail varnish, no jewellery)
- good personal hygiene habits (e.g. no licking fingers, tasting with a clean teaspoon)
- safe use of equipment, especially knives, pans and electrical equipment
- selection of the correct tools (e.g. correct knife for chopping, peeling)
- use of a wide variety of commodities within the task chosen
- good food hygiene (e.g. perishable foods refrigerated, not left on work unit/table, using temperature probes to ensure food is cooked)
- neat, organised work
- safe use of oven and hob
- working to time
- independent working
- good technical skills
- little food waste
- logical sequence of work, e.g. food that needs to be cooked for a long time, be set or served cold needs to be made first
- a wide variety of skills, including high-level skills
- high standard of final presentation, e.g. portion control, use of garnish and decoration, good colour, correct temperature, correct texture, good flavour, appropriate serving dishes

- good sequencing and dovetailing of dishes so that all elements of the meal are served at the correct temperatures
- appropriate serving of the meal.

Evaluating the task (15 marks)

In order to gain high marks in this section you need to discuss:

- the suitability of the meal chosen
- any changes you would make to the choice of dishes and why
- time management
- how customers (consumers) would regard your dishes in terms of appearance, flavour and texture
- what improvements you would make and why
- the size and cost per portion
- selling price and profit margins
- the nutritional content of the meal with valid comments.

Note: Remember that your research does not need to be presented in a written format. However, you must produce photographs of displays, computer printouts, results of questionnaires, photographs of trialled recipes, leaflets, etc. as evidence that you have carried out the research.

Choosing dishes

Choosing the right dishes to make for a practical is one of the most difficult tasks. Try to include a variety of colours, textures and flavours.

Also, try to choose dishes that show skill, such as:

- rubbing-in, e.g. pastry, crumble, biscuits
- creaming, e.g. fairy cakes, pineapple upside-down pudding, piped biscuits
- whisking, e.g. gateau
- sauce-making, e.g. béchamel or custard
- yeast mixtures, e.g. pizza or bread rolls
- dishes using high-risk foods like meat, chicken and fish, e.g. chicken chasseur, lasagne.

Try also to make some dishes that show a variety of cooking methods, such as boiling, baking, frying, grilling. A careful choice of dishes means you will get off to a good start with your task.

Lasagne

Reasons for your choice

Read the following. Use only those that are relevant:

1. Dishes show a variety of **colours** (state the colours of each dish – remember to avoid all cream, brown or green).
2. Dishes show a variety of **textures** (chewy, soft, crunchy, crisp, etc.).
3. Cost – state if the dishes are economical, if you are using food in season, if you are using a wide or basic range of commodities. (For the commodity task refer to your research.)
4. Time taken to prepare and cook. All dishes should 'fit' into the given time (consider setting time as well as cooking or cooling time).

5. Sale-able. Customers in a restaurant would be willing to pay.

6. Easy to control portions and serve. State how you will portion all dishes, i.e. use of garnish or decoration, use of spoons, ladles, etc.

7. Dishes will look attractive (explain garnish/decoration which will help the dishes 'stand out').

8. Dishes show a range of skill. You must include at least one high-level (hands-on) skill, e.g. pastry, cake, biscuit, scone, bread, sauce mixture.

9. Dishes show a variety of cooking methods (baking, frying, grilling, boiling).

10. Dishes should be suitable for given groups (when preparing meals for children, vegetarians, old people or ethnic groups).

11. Healthy eating – where possible, include dishes that are low in fat, sugar and salt and high in fibre, i.e. include wholemeal products, cereals, fresh fruit and vegetables, to reflect current thinking on nutrition.

12. All your dishes should be suitable for producing in bulk.

13. Where appropriate, dishes should be suitable for refrigerating/freezing for use another time, and kept hot (above 63°C) or reheated safely. (Note: Reheated food should not be served to high-risk groups.)

14. Make reference to personal hygiene and critical control points – how you will prepare yourself, where you will take extra hygiene/safety precautions (e.g. preparation of chicken – keep refrigerated, handle as little as possible, cook thoroughly, wash equipment and hands thoroughly to prevent cross contamination).

Writing a time plan

When you have decided on your menu or choice of dishes, your next task is to write your time plan. Many students have found the following method helpful. Although it takes a lot of time to start with, it makes sure that you don't miss out any of the stages.

> **Menu**
> Chicken chasseur
> Creamed potatoes
> Peas
> Strawberry gateau

First, go through each dish and make a numbered list of all the stages in making each one, from mise-en-place through to serving.

An example is given below for the chosen menu.

Example stages for time plan

Chicken chasseur

1. Skin chicken, peel and chop vegetables.
2. Fry chicken. Remove from pan.
3. Fry onion and bacon, add flavour and the rest of the ingredients for sauce.
4. Re-add chicken and simmer on hob for 45 mins.
5. Place chicken in serving dish.
6. Garnish and serve.

Strawberry gateau

1. Make sponge base (whisk eggs and sugar till thick, fold in flour). Bake Gas 6/200°C for 15–20 mins.
2. Turn onto wire rack and allow to cool.
3. Whip cream and cut strawberries.
4. Decorate gateau and refrigerate (portion control).
5. Serve.

Creamed potatoes

1. Peel and chop potatoes, cover with fresh cold water.
2. Salt – bring to boil.
3. Simmer for 20 mins.
4. Drain – mash with butter and milk.
5. Place in serving dish, level top and fork round.
6. Garnish and serve.

Peas

1. Place peas in boiling water.
2. Simmer for 7–10 mins.
3. Drain – add butter.
4. Serve.

You then need to 'dovetail' each stage of each dish to make a time plan, as shown in the example below. Start your plan with the dishes that need the longest cooking time, cooling time or setting time. Finish with the final garnish and serving. Allow at least 10 minutes for final garnish and decoration before serving. Make sure you start and finish tasks at the correct times.

Time plan

Time	Order of work	Special points
8.30	Mise-en-place. Set up table. Collect serving dishes. Peel and chop potatoes. Prepare garnishes and decorations (whip cream, fan strawberries). Chop parsley. Peel and chop onion, dice bacon, chop mushrooms. Tidy table for start.	Refrigerate perishables (chicken and cream). Light oven – Gas 6 or 200°C.
9.00	Gateau: Make sponge using whisking method. (Whisk eggs and sugar till thick, fold in flour.) Divide between two tins.	Fold in gently. Bake – 20 mins.
9.20	Chicken chasseur: Fry chicken to seal. Remove and place on plate. Fry bacon and onion, add flour, tomatoes, stock, puree etc. Re-add chicken pieces and mushrooms. Simmer.	Use tongs to turn chicken. Very low heat for at least 45 mins.
9.40	Check gateau base – remove from oven if cooked. Turn onto wire rack.	Should feel 'springy' in centre.
9.45	Wash up. Put potatoes on to boil. When boiling, reduce the heat and simmer. Stir chasseur.	Add tsp salt. Simmer 20 mins on low heat.
9.55	Decorate gateau with swirls of cream and fanned strawberries.	Remember portion control. Refrigerate.
10.05	Wash up. Boil water in kettle for peas.	
10.10	Put peas in pan. Add boiling water. Simmer for 7–10 minutes.	Medium heat.
10.15	Check potatoes – if cooked drain and mash with butter and milk. Spread in dish. Fork round, garnish with sprig of parsley.	Cold water soak for pans. Place in oven to keep hot.

Time	Order of work	Special points
10.20	Drain peas. Place in serving dish. Place chasseur in serving dish and garnish with a row of parsley.	Wipe edges of dishes.
10.25	Take gateau from fridge. Place on table with main course dishes.	
10.30	Serve all dishes. Complete washing up.	

Shopping list

The shopping list for your assessment must be written accurately in order to gain full marks. You must identify food correctly (e.g. caster sugar, **plain** flour, **block** margarine) and give the total amounts needed.

Use all metric quantities.

Using the following headings may help you identify the different commodities more easily:

- Butcher/Fishmonger.
- Grocer.
- Greengrocer.
- Dairy.

Under the heading of Greengrocer, group foods into vegetables, salad, fruit and fresh herbs.

REMEMBER

Remember to include all garnishes and decorations on your shopping list.

Equipment list

List the equipment you need to carry out your assessment under three headings:

1. Preparation.
2. Special equipment.
3. Serving dishes.

Heading 1 (Preparation) should contain all the equipment you need to make and cook your dishes, including bowls, knives, piping bags, baking trays, etc.

Heading 2 (Special equipment) should list any special equipment you need (especially as it is limited in some rooms), e.g. microwave, toaster, hand-held mixer.

Heading 3 (Serving dishes) should list all the serving dishes, flats, vegetable dishes and cake stands that you need. Also include here any paper doilies and dish papers.

You should not have to use more than one or two items of the same type (e.g. mixing bowls). If you do this you will have too much washing up, and (more important) you will lose marks!

Evaluation

When carrying out your evaluation, consider each of the following:

1. **Suitability** of dishes chosen: what dishes did you make? Why were they suitable for the task?

2. Did you include a variety of **cooking skills**, e.g. sauce making, pastry making, bread making, rubbing in, creaming, whisking? State what skills you used for each dish.

3. Did you include a variety of **cooking methods**, i.e. boiling, baking, toasting, frying, poaching, microwaving? State what methods of cooking you used for each dish.

4. Comment on your **time management** during the task.

5. **Customer acceptability**: make comments about appearance, flavour and texture of each dish (you must taste your food), correct number of portions, portion size, use the correct sized dishes for amounts of food, attractive garnish or decoration, whether food was hot, cold or set as needed and the effect of the 'whole' table. Would your food be acceptable for paying customers?

6. Suggest any **improvements** you would make given the same task again. If you would choose a different dish(es), say what you would choose and why.

7. If you could improve the 'making' say how and why.

8. If you would improve the presentation or change the order of work suggest how and why.

9. Calculate and comment on **cost per** portion and **portion size**.

10. For Task 2 only: Work out the **nutritional content** of the meal (using food tables or a computer programme).

REMEMBER

Don't use the word 'nice' in your evaluation – it's too general. Try to find words that describe the food and your work more clearly.

Comment on the nutritional value of the dishes or meal as appropriate for the task. For example if you are preparing a meal for a vegetarian explain the protein content of the meal. Vegetarians often lack iron and vitamin B so explain how you could boost their content.

11. Work out the selling price and comment on profit margins you would expect to make if working in a commercial establishment.

Calculating selling price

The 'selling price' of food is calculated (worked out) according to the amount of profit that an establishment wants to make. This is because the selling price has to take into account:

- the actual food cost (the cost of the ingredients)
- overheads (the cost of rates, gas, electricity, etc.)
- labour cost (staff wages)
- profit
- VAT.

The selling price can be calculated as follows:

Food cost $\times$ 100 $\div$ 40

Example: If food costs were £4 the calculation would be:

4 (food cost) $\times$ 100 $\div$ 40 (required profit)

400 $\div$ 40 = 10

The selling price would be £10.

Anglia Hotel Restaurant	
Registered office: Anglia Road, Cambridge CB1 1XY	
Your server was: Robert	
2 Sparkling water 1 litre	£5.98
1 Orange juice	£1.45
2 Soup	£6.20
1 Risotto	£7.00
1 Roast pork	£9.75
1 Cheesecake	£3.00
2 Espresso	£6.00
Total	£39.38
Service charge not included	
Thank you for visiting Anglia Hotel Restaurant	

A simple way of calculating selling price is to multiply the food costs by 3.

Example: If food costs were £4 the calculation would be:

$$4 \times 3 = 12$$

The selling price woud be £12.

Always remember to use the correct mathematical calculation. Some food costs are in £ and therefore involve a simple calculation. Some food costs are in pence, so you need to use a decimal point.

Sample calculations

If food costs were £2.50, the calculation would be:

$$2.50 \times 100 \div 40 = 6.25 \text{ (i.e. £6.25)}.$$

If food costs were 60p the calculation would be:

$$60 \times 100 \div 40 = 1.50 \text{ (i.e. £1.50)}.$$

This unit is assessed through a written paper and is worth 40 per cent of your final grade for a single award in Catering, or 20 per cent of a double award in Hospitality and Catering.

The paper lasts for 1¼ hours and will have a range of questions covering all the areas you have learnt throughout the course and through carrying out your practical tasks. The start of the paper will be assessed through recall of knowledge. The questions towards the middle and end of the paper will ask for more detailed answers to demonstrate your understanding. The catering examination will be available either as an electronic assessment or as a traditional written paper. Some examples of questions and answers are set out at the end of this book. Familiarisation tests and sample assessment questions are available on the WJEC website.

If you want to earn high marks for the longer questions at the end of the paper you should answer the questions fully, giving relevant facts, examples and explanations.

GCSE HOSPITALITY (SINGLE AWARD)

3.1 THE HOSPITALITY INDUSTRY

The hospitality industry includes a wide range of establishments providing accommodation and food services. These can be in the commercial or non-commercial (catering services) sector.

Examples include:

- **commercial establishments:** pubs, bistros, cafes, restaurants, fast-food outlets, restaurants, hostels, bed and breakfast, caravan parks and holiday resorts. These establishments charge the customers for the services they provide and therefore make a profit.
- **non-commercial (catering services) establishments:** hospitals, schools, prisons, colleges, universities, the armed forces and care homes all need food and drink although hospitality is not the main focus. These establishments often run on a limited budget and do not make a profit, but supply a service to support the communities. Contract catering also falls into this sector. Contract catering companies bid for a contract to run catering services in an establishment such as a school. The company that wins the contract will then provide the catering for a fixed period of time.

The hospitality industry is important because it:

- is a national employment provider
- benefits the local economy
- has important links to leisure, travel and tourism.

Hospitality is the fastest growing industry in the UK and covers a vast area of employment. There are over 2 and a half million people employed in the industry in the UK. Most employees are British but over 40 per cent are from other countries. Many establishments will try to employ local staff; however, there is a shortage of staff available so some jobs are advertised abroad. The quality of training courses offered in the UK also means that people come to Britain to study and many British people are employed in prestigious placements abroad.

The hospitality industry has links with tourism as people travel for work or pleasure and they require food, drink and sometimes accommodation. Overseas visitors spend one third of the cost of their holiday on accommodation and catering. Tourists also visit attractions such as theme parks, historic buildings, art galleries, scenic places and special events. During these visits, sectors such as accommodation and catering may be in great demand. However, the number of tourists can fall if the weather is bad or there are increased risks to health and safety, for example an outbreak of disease or act of terrorism.

Organisations in the industry

There are several organisations involved in the industry:

- Institute of Hospitality
- RIPH – Royal Institute of Public Health
- CIEH – Chartered Institute of Environmental Health
- SSC – Sector Skills Council
- People 1st – Sector skills council for hospitality, leisure and travel and tourism
- BHA – British Hospitality Association
- BII – British Instiute of Inn-Keeping
- RSPH – Royal Society for the Promotion of Health.

Many of these organisations set and promote standards of safety, management and education in the hospitality, tourism and leisure industries.

ACTIVITY

Look at the list of organisations here.

- Which ones are linked to food safety and hygiene?
- Which ones are linked to standards of service?
- Which ones are linked to staffing?

Sectors within the industry

Within the industry there is a range of sectors and it is important to understand how these sectors work and for whom they provide a service.

The main sectors of the hospitality and catering industry are:

- Accommodation. Some areas of the hospitality industry provide accommodation, shelter, food, drink and sometimes entertainment to the customer, for example holiday parks, hotels and resorts.
- Food and beverages. This sector prepares and serves food and drink to the customer. Outlets include fast-food outlets, cafes, restaurants, public houses and contract caterers.
- Meetings and events. Some establishments provide rooms to hold meetings and events. They may also provide food and drink for the clients and some also provide accommodation. These are known as 'conference facilities'. Clients specify what kind of service they require, e.g. boardroom-style meeting room with lunch and refreshments served at given times.
- Entertainment and leisure. This sector includes leisure facilities, golf clubs, racetracks, cinemas and bowling alleys. People often want food and drink when they attend these establishments and this sector meets those needs.
- Travel and tourism services: There is a strong link between the hospitality industry and travel and tourism. Customers who are travelling by plane, boat, coach or car all require food and drink on the journey.

Employment providers

Establishments within the hospitality and catering sectors all provide employment for the community they are in. The company may also buy local produce for the meals and services they provide. We are being encouraged to cut down our carbon footprint and the amount of miles that food goods travel, so it is beneficial to the local community if the establishment buys local produce and uses local services such as electricians, florists and plumbers. Hospitality establishments may include information about locally grown or reared produce that feature on their menus to encourage customers to buy them.

Employment opportunities

Workers employed by the companies could be full-time, part-time or casual staff.

- **Full-time staff** have permanent jobs in the establishment and work all year. They should have a contract with their terms of employment set out in writing. They could work set shifts or shifts that change daily depending on how busy the establishment is. They will often work a set amount of days over a seven-day week, including weekends.
- **Part-time staff** may work on set days of the week, or have set shifts. They may be employed permanently, but do fewer hours a week than full-time staff, often working during the busier times of the day such as service of meals.
- **Casual staff** work for specific functions and are often employed through an agency. They do not have a contract or set hours to work, but are called in during busier times of the year, such as Christmas. Often, casual staff work for the same establishment each year as they know their way round and know how the company works. However, this is not always the case and some casual staff do not know where they will be working until the week before.

Links with travel and tourism

The hospitality industry links well with the travel and tourism industry as they both provide a customer service. Visitors to the area often require a place to stay overnight and somewhere to eat and drink. The tourism industry links with the hospitality industry to provide a service to the customer, giving information about the establishments that have the facilities the customer needs. This could include being close to attractions or having leisure facilities available for the customer.

ACTIVITY

Choose a local establishment and find out whether or not they employ local staff and use local produce and services. Make a list or table to show your findings.

Types of service provided include:

- **Accommodation.** Customers may require accommodation for one or more nights. This accommodation can be a basic single or double room with en suite facilities or a more luxurious room or suite. The cost of the accommodation will vary depending on the facilities in the room. Customers often request internet access, which will be charged at an hourly or daily rate. They may ask for a shower rather than a bath or they may require facilities for disabled guests. Most rooms provide tea- and coffee-making equipment and some may have a mini bar and additional equipment such as a trouser press.

  Hotels have different price rates for their rooms (see left). Companies that hold conferences or use the hotel regularly may be given a special rate.

- **Full meals.** Customers may require full meals for breakfast, lunch and dinner. These meals can be provided in the restaurant area, or in hotel rooms through room service. Full meals may be selected from a set menu, choice from a table d'hôte menu or from an à la carte menu. Customers will have a choice of starter dishes, main course dishes and desserts on a lunch and dinner menu.

  Breakfast may include continental breakfast, full English or a 'mix and match' or buffet service as well as cereals and drinks. Many establishments now offer a buffet style lunch where there is a choice of dishes available and customers serve themselves. This cuts down on the need for additional staff, especially during conferences, which may run beyond the set time for lunch. Customers holding an event, for example, a wedding or birthday party, will arrange a set menu for the event with a few choices of pre-ordered dishes. Many pubs now offer food all day and many have snack and full meal menus for the customer to choose from. Some establishments also have 'meal deals', where customers get the cheapest meal free. Many restaurants offer children's meals and 'mix and match' children's meals where the customers can choose the food to suit their tastes and dietary needs.

Hotel rates

- Rack rate: the rate offered to customers who approach the hotel directly. Displayed in reception. Not discounted.
- Business rate: for business customers.
- Internet rate: for customers who book online. Often cheaper than rack rate.

● Snacks, including tea and coffee. Some customers may only require snacks and drinks to be served at specific times during the day. Many establishments offer self-service coffee and tea facilities so that customers can help themselves and these are available all day. Some establishments may have a snack menu, usually at the bar where customers can order snacks rather than meals. Cafeterias offer both snacks and meals at all times.

● Conference facilities. Often, businesses and groups require a place to hold a meeting or conference. Many hospitality establishments offer this facility. Meeting rooms are available in a range of sizes and they may hold from 6 to over 100 delegates (people attending the conference). The rooms can be set out in a range of styles, such as boardroom (see right), where all delegates can see each other; theatre, with rows of seats, so everyone can watch a presentation; cabaret, with small tables for groups of delegates to work together and communicate with each other; or top table (see right), with the most important people facing everyone else.

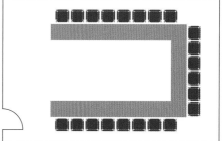

Top table layout

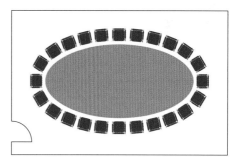

Boardroom layout

Companies who are holding conferences may also require snacks and drinks on arrival, and lunch. Some delegates may require accommodation if they have travelled some distance. Water and pens and paper are needed on the tables. The person delivering the meeting may require an overhead projector and screen, computer facilities, a flip chart and pens to enable them to demonstrate points to the delegates. Hotels usually charge a 'daily delegate rate' for these facilities.

● Function facilities. Customers may also require a room to hold a function such as a wedding reception. Many establishments offer these facilities. The cost will include the hire of the room and the customer's other requirements. Customers may want to bring their own food and music. Some establishments allow this, others do not. For example, church halls may charge for the room rental and customers can provide their own food, made by themselves or a contract caterer. Hotels usually offer an 'all-in' price for the room and food. They often recommend someone to provide music. Pubs may offer the room alone, or the room and food. Costs vary depending on the establishment and its facilities. Room layout styles will be similar to those of conferences, e.g. top table style.

ACTIVITY

Find out about different establishments in your area that have function facilities. Choose an event such as a birthday party and suggest which establishment would provide best value for money, giving reasons for your choice.

Client group

There is a range of client groups who require different services from the industry.

Businesses often use facilities and services in relation to work, such as conference facilities, food and accommodation for meetings, training sessions and other courses. These services are usually paid for by the business. They may use contract caterers to provide food and drinks for in-house meetings.

Private: this is where a customer's individual demands are met. Private events may include weddings and parties and can be held in a variety of establishments, such as hotels, restaurants, local venues or at home.

Groups include tourists, associations, clubs, etc. They have a variety of catering requirements. For example, the 'Young Farmers' group may want outdoor catering, such as a barbeque. Some customers have special requirements because of their culture or dietary needs. Customers can also be grouped into ages, i.e. children, young people, adults, elderly people. Each group will have their own needs.

ACTIVITY

Find out about the different types of hospitality establishments in your area and match them with the type of client group they provide for. How many can you find?

Job roles

There is a range of jobs available in the hospitality industry.

They can be split into three main groups:

- management and administration
- front-of-house
- accommodation.

Within each of these groups there are various jobs. Let's look briefly at each area.

Management

There may be a manager for all the different areas of a large establishment, but only one in a smaller place. Within a larger company there may be:

- a manager, who is in charge of the day-to-day running of the company, and is responsible for making a profit and organising every area.
- an assistant manager, who is responsible to the manager and may have work delegated to him by the manager. He/she will also be in charge in the manager's absence.

Front-of-house

Again, depending on the size of the establishment, this role may be taken on by the owner, or staff will be employed to do it. Front-of-house roles include:

- the head receptionist, who is responsible for taking the bookings and ensuring the staff are given the correct information. The receptionist is the first person the customer comes into contact with. They help customers check in, and deal with any complaints. They inform other departments about room bookings, and may also complete staff rotas and deliver staff training.
- the assistant receptionist, who assists the head receptionist, helps customers to check in, deals with bills and answers the phone.

- the porter, who delivers cases to rooms and helps in setting up rooms for conferences etc.
- the night porter, who covers the reception at night and ensures any complaints or queries are dealt with effectively.
- administrative staff, who deal with the day-to-day running of the hotel, internet bookings, maintenance, laundry services and any incidents that may arise.
- concierge, who move customer's cars, help with booking trips and theatre tickets, call taxis and look after luggage.

Accommodation services

These are the staff who look after the rooms that are available to hire and include:

- Head housekeeper, who is responsible for ensuring all the rooms are ready for customers, compiles rotas for staff, ensures staff are aware of what rooms need to be cleaned and checks laundry.
- Housekeeper, who is responsible for allocating jobs to chambermaids, checking laundry and toiletries, checking rooms are cleaned correctly.
- Room attendant, who cleans the rooms, changes the beds, and checks toiletries, towels, etc. are filled.
- Maintenance officer, who completes any repairs that can be done in- house, gets specialist maintenance staff in, e.g. gas engineer, when required.

Conference managers

These managers are responsible for organising conferences and events to be held at the establishment. When a customer makes enquiries about holding an event/conference they speak to the conference manager, who will arrange a meeting. At this meeting the customer will tell the manager the date and time of the event, how many people will be attending and the sort of facilities that are required. The conference manager will keep in touch with the customer at frequent intervals to check that the requirements have not changed. For example they will need to know of any special dietary needs of the guests. Prior to the event the conference manager will ensure all staff are booked and that the room is set out to the needs of the customer. On the day of the event they will meet the customer and brief them on the fire and safety regulations.

They will be available throughout the event to answer any questions and to sort out any problems that may arise.

Working together

Within the hospitality industry it is important for all areas to work together. It is impossible for any department to function entirely on its own. If one department fails to complete its functions, guests may be disappointed with the services.

Think about what happens when a guest arrives at a hotel.

● Housekeeping must prepare the room and let reception know it is ready for the customers.
● Maintenance may have completed some repairs that were reported by the room attendant.
● Concierge are the first to greet the guests when they arrive at the hotel and tell them about trips and events close by.
● Reception are contacted if the guests need any special equipment, such as a baby's cot.
● The porter assists the guests with their luggage.
● Room service is available for guests who arrive late and have missed dinner.
● The restaurant staff are notified by reception what time the guests would like to eat.

All this may have occurred because the administrative staff have developed and advertised a special weekend deal for families.

Career paths

There are many career paths within the industry and a range of jobs can be found in the different sectors. For example, a person could be employed in the kitchen of a restaurant and then move to a hotel and progress from there into management.

Most people who go into the hospitality and catering industry are able to work their way up to the position they would like. It is a great industry to be involved in and you can often meet famous people on the way. Larger establishments offer the opportunity to work in a range of areas and provide training on the job. The advantage of this is you can earn at the same time. You can also go on day release or attend college full time.

Working in the hospitality industry gives you the opportunity to travel if you wish to. Jobs are available locally, nationally and internationally. Jobs are often advertised in local newspapers and in magazines such as *The Caterer and Hotelkeeper*, *The Grocer* and *The Journal of Hospitality and Tourism Management*. It is very easy to find out the jobs that are available through job centres, the press and websites. Many larger companies and chains advertise jobs on their websites. They are often updated regularly so it is worth checking daily. Also, your local college will have links with various hotels and restaurants and could be a good source of knowledge when it comes to applying for jobs.

Receptionist, Anglia Hotel

Cambridge
Live in
Competitive salary, dependant upon experience

In this role you will assist customers from booking to check out. At the Anglia Hotel, we offer five star service.

We are looking for someone who is passionate about hospitality. Previous experience is essential.

You will work 5 days out of 7, in straight shifts, early and late. Meals will be provided when on duty. Uniform also provided. We offer an excellent package of benefits, and you will receive a share of the service charge earned.

TERMINOLOGY:

Management: the people who are in charge of specific areas.

Front-of-house: the reception area of the establishment.

Accommodation services: the housekeeping side of an establishment.

ACTIVITY

Find out what jobs are available in your area. Research how you can progress up the ladder and what qualifications you would need to be able to do the job.

With the help of your teacher, carry out a mock interview for a job you would like to do.

List the personal skills you would need to work in the hospitality and catering industry.

Planning an event-based function

When planning a function the following must be considered:

- Date and time of event
- Choice of venue and booking
- Number of guests
- Menu and type of service
- Costing
- Promotion (advertising)
- Décor and presentation
- Room layout and table layout
- Menu cards and place cards
- Staffing
- Risk assessment.

Date and time of event

Plan the event well in advance. The date and time must be suitable for the organisers as well as the guests.

Choice of venue and booking

Consider where the event will be held, as rooms may need to be booked in advance. Look at areas within the workplace that are big enough and discuss the pros and cons of holding an event in these places.

You are invited to a

SPRING LUNCH

Albany School hall

Tuesday 3rd April

12 o'clock

RSVP

Number of guests

The number might be large or small. If there is a small number of people preparing for an event, they cannot cater for and serve a very large number of guests. Consider the time taken to cook and serve the food. Guests will need time to eat and time to socialise.

Menu and type of service

The type of event will determine the type of menu.

Table d'hôte This is a set menu for a set price. This type of menu may have a selection of starters, main course and dessert. The customer then selects which one they would prefer. There is usually a vegetarian option on the menu.

À la carte This is a selection of courses, all priced individually and cooked to order. This menu usually has a wider choice for the customer for each course and may include a fish course and wider selection for vegetarians.

Take-aways These menus give a list of various products (e.g. pizzas, Chinese dishes) that are available at set prices. They are not eaten on the premises and may be delivered to the home.

Children's meals Children's meals are often on a separate menu that is more colourful and may include a theme. The choices available are limited and often now include a healthier option or multiple choices so the parents can make up the meal to suit the needs of the child.

Set menu for a function These menus usually have a choice for the customer and they may then chose one option for all guests or ask each guest what they require from a limited choice. These are often used for sit-down functions or for buffets where the clients choose the meal for a set price per person.

Fast food/café These menus have a choice of quick-to-prepare foods at set prices. The foods may range from snacks, sandwiches and cakes, to a full dinner or breakfast. They also include drinks that can be bought alone or with the meal or snack.

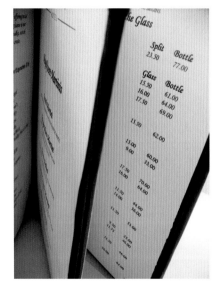

Things to consider when planning a menu

The following points should be considered when planning a menu:

- colour
- texture
- flavour
- the skills you have
- temperature

- time
- foods in season
- cost
- customer needs
- the occasion
- the type of menu.

Colour, flavour and texture

There is a saying that 'people eat with their eyes'. Food should look appetising to the customer. It should include a range of contrasting flavours, but not so many that the customer cannot taste the main product. The complete meal should have a range of textures (e.g. smooth, crunchy).

Chicken and vegetables provide different colours, flavours and textures

Skills, temperature and time

Choose recipes that can be made successfully. Think about the equipment available in the kitchen. Check the time it takes to cook the product and the oven temperatures. The oven may have to be used for more than one dish, so check the temperatures for each product to see if it is possible to complete the meal.

Foods in season and cost

Consider the foods that are available and their cost. Most foods are available all year now, but may be more expensive if they have been imported – for example, strawberries are cheaper to buy in June and July as they are available in the UK, but they are available all year if imported. Cost the meal according to the ingredients you purchase.

Customer needs, occasion and type of menu

Consider customers' needs and any special dietary requirements they may have. The type of occasion will affect the type of menu. For example, at a charity event where pizza is sold by the slice a selection of three or four types of pizza might need to be available. A meal to celebrate a wedding anniversary will need a balanced three- or four-course menu, taking into account special dietary needs.

Trialling recipes

It is a good idea to trial any new recipes before running an event. If there are any problems, the recipe can be adapted or changed.

Preparation and presentation of food

- Soups – should be served hot, in hot bowls on a side plate. Always add some garnish before serving and ensure that bowls are not too full. Use a ladle to ensure accurate portion control.
- Starters (hot and cold) – these portions should not be too big, as customers should not be too full to enjoy the rest of the meal. Remember that is only a starter! Hot starters should be served on hot plates and cold starters on cold plates. Add a garnish to enhance the look of the product. Starters such as prawn cocktail should be served with brown bread and butter.
- Main courses (including vegetarian options) – an average serving is 200g of meat or protein product and 200g of vegetables. Do not overload the plate and ensure that all portions are the same. Garnish such as a side salad can be added to meats such as steak and chicken. Fish dishes can be served with a wedge or slice of lemon and some parsley to enhance the look of the dish.
- Accompaniments – this refers to vegetables, starchy foods, such as rice, potatoes and pasta, and sauces and gravies.
- Desserts (hot and cold) – individual portions should be served and should be consistent in size. Cold desserts should be served on cold plates and hot desserts on hot plates.
- Beverages (non alcoholic) – if you are serving non-alcoholic wine alternatives such as Schloer, use the appropriate wine glasses as if serving alcoholic wine. Water should be cold and served in wine goblets or tumblers. Fruit juices should be served in wine goblets whenever possible. Ensure that tea and coffee are piping hot and that the tea is not stewed. Coffee should be served with cream or milk and a choice of brown or white sugar.

REMEMBER

Remember that the plate you serve food on is like an artist's canvas. White plates look better than coloured plates and show off the food better. Always clean the edge of the plate and ensure the food looks its best before serving.

- Snack dishes/meals – these are smaller portions and can be served on breakfast plates. When serving sandwiches it is always advisable to add a small side salad to enhance the look of the dish.

Food not presented well

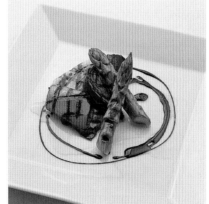

Food presented well

Food and beverage service equipment

One of the main pieces of equipment used in the restaurant is the wait station or dumb waiter. This is a unit with cupboards and drawers to hold spare cutlery and crockery, as well as any condiments needed. The top should be kept as clear as possible as this gives somewhere to put dirty equipment while clearing tables. Spare folded napkins and menus, including children's menus, are also stored here.

A restaurant wait station

Many restaurants use an electronic point of sale (EPOS) order system. The waiting staff take the order and enter it into the computer at the wait station. The order is then transferred to the kitchen staff who prepare the order. At the end of service the customer's details and table number are entered into the computer and the bill is generated automatically. This system is becoming increasingly popular as it avoids confusion and mistakes can be easily monitored.

Other pieces of equipment used in food service areas include coffee machines, Gueridon trolleys and hotplates.

How to serve customers correctly

Before guests arrive, make sure that all tables are set correctly and no cutlery is missing. Check that all knives are facing inwards and that cutlery is straight. Ensure that napkins are set out correctly and all the condiments are ready for the meal.

When customers arrive, the first thing staff should do is to make them welcome and show them to their seats. This is called 'greeting and seating'. This is usually the restaurant manager's responsibility.

A seating plan for guests can help when serving the meals. Make sure that staff stick to the seating plan to avoid disruption later.

Customers should be asked what they would like to drink. Check if they have pre-ordered, and if they have not, give them the menu. When staff return with the drinks they should ask if the customers are ready to order. Staff should be polite at all times. When taking the order staff should stand to the left of the customer. They need to be familiar with all the dishes on the menu and be prepared to answer any questions about the meal.

Serving food

As a general rule women and older people should be served first. Some establishments serve food from the left and clear from the right; others do the opposite. However, drinks should be served from the right whenever possible. Staff should be polite and attentive throughout service. They need to carry out a 'satisfaction check' with the customer within the first few minutes to check that all is well with the meal.

Customer service

Customers want to enjoy their meal experience and event organisers want them to come back.

When dealing with guests with special needs or guests who are very young, elderly or disabled, staff should do their best to meet the needs of these guests, just as they would for any other. Make sure that older guests do not have to walk far to get to their table. Make sure that those who are

REMEMBER

Serve from the left and clear from the right whenever possible.

REMEMBER

All guests are equal and staff should strive to treat them all in the same way. Each situation, no matter how unpleasant or unusual, shoud be handled with care and consideration.

disabled have enough room to move, especially if they are in a wheelchair.

If a customer complains, handle the situation calmly and courteously. Stay professional and never blame someone else. Remember the customer is always right.

This is a good way to handle complaints:

● Listen to the details of the complaint.
● Repeat the complaint briefly to show you understand the problem.
● Handle the complaint promptly.
● Make an immediate adjustment if you can.
● Apologise.
● Always treat the customer in the way that you would like to be treated yourself.

REMEMBER

A happy customer = a returning customer = more profit!

Ways in which customer service can be measured

Customer care can be assessed either by verbal or written feedback from the customer or by observation from staff.

Costing and portion control

When costing dishes, consider:

● the cost of the ingredients – keep copies of till receipts or website print-outs; note any special offers, or ingredients that are free
● the amount of the ingredients used
● the cost of the amount used.

When calculating a selling price, the following costs need to be considered:

● food costs
● overheads, e.g. electricity and gas
● staff wages
● profit
● VAT.

Most companies try to make a 60 per cent gross profit on the initial cost of the food, to cover all the other costs. However, an easy way to calculate a selling price is to multiply the food costs by three.

AS A GUIDE, YOU CAN GENERALLY ALLOW THE FOLLOWING:

- Soup – 4–6 portions per litre
- Meat – 6–8 portions per kg
- Cold meat – 16 portions per kg
- Potatoes – 8 portions per kg
- Vegetables – 6–8 portions per kg
- Sauces – 8–12 portions per 0.5 litre

An individual beef and onion pie

A portion of soup and bread

How can you achieve effective portion control?

- Use dishes that are the same size when cooking the product (e.g. pizza).
- Weigh the ingredients and allow a certain amount per person.
- Use plates that are the same size when serving the product.
- Use spoons that are the same size for serving the product.
- Show portion control in the decoration of a product, e.g. gateau.
- Use scoops for ice cream or potatoes.
- Use ladles for soup and sauces.
- Use individual pie dishes.

All customers should be served the same size portion. Children and older people tend to eat less than women, and men tend to eat more than women, so take this into account when considering portion sizes.

Other points to consider are:

- the quality of the food – better quality food yields a greater number of portions
- the cost of the food – this should be related to the quality of the food.

Promotion

Possible ways to promote an event include:

- Invitations
- Questionnaires
- Posters
- Flyers
- Advertisements in newspapers, magazines, websites, radio or television.

Décor and presentation

Consider themes and colour schemes. For example, the venue for a pizza event could be decorated with Italian flags or have a red, green and wite colour scheme. The venue for a golden wedding anniversary party could be decorated in gold and white or cream.

Room and table layout

The room needs to be set up to suit the type of event and the type of guests. There are several ways of arranging the tables for an event (see Section 3.2).

Table setting

The type of menu will affect how the table is laid.

Learn the correct terminology used when laying tables. In the hospitality industry, a place setting for one person is called a cover. The bread and butter knife is usually place on the left-hand side of the place setting.

1 Butter knife
2 Bread–and–butter plate
3 Soup spoon (first course)
4 Seafood fork (second course)
5 Seafood knife (second course)
6 Meat and salad fork (main course)
7 Dinner knife (main course)
8 Decoration plate
9 Soup bowl
10 Dessert spoon
11 Dessert fork
12 Water glass
13 Champagne glass
14 Wine glass (for red)
15 Wine glass (for white)

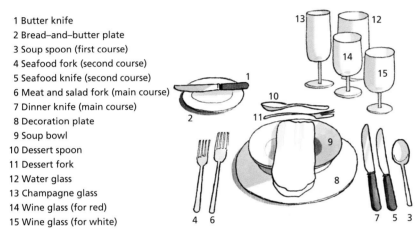

Place setting

Menu cards and place cards

Menu cards can add to the overall appearance of the table and impression of the establishment, or detract from them, so it is important to get them right. The menu should be easy to read, even in dim light. If the dishes are named in a foreign language or are not self-explanatory, a short description of each dish should be included.

Place cards are used at functions and large events such as weddings. They should match the menu cards.

Staffing

Several job roles may be needed to run a successful event. These are described on the following pages. Good teamwork is essential when holding an event.

ACTIVITY

- Look at some examples of café and restaurant menus. What font size is used? What colours are used? Are pictures included? Are the menus large, small, folded or shaped?
- Design a menu for a Hallowe'en party.

Front-of-house staff

Front-of-house staff are the first people the customers come in contact with. First impressions are important, so front-of-house staff need to be well presented and friendly.

Roles within the front-of-house team include:

- administrative procedures – filing, processing enquiries
- billing of customers – payment
- booking systems – procedures and recording
- communication – talking, listening, writing, reading, giving and receiving information
- customer care – welcome, body language, politeness
- ICT skills – database, word-processing skills
- storage of personal data – governed by the Data Protection Act.

Accommodation staff

- Conference Manager – organises conferences and events held at the establishment.
- Housekeeper – allocates jobs to chambermaids, supervises and checks standards, deals with customer complaints.
- Room attendants/chambermaids – clean and service the rooms ready for the guests and prepare for meetings and functions.
- Porters – carry out heavy duties, e.g. moving furniture, carrying luggage.
- Cleaners – carry out the daily general cleaning of the public areas, and special preparation and cleaning for functions and business events.

Kitchen staff

- Head Chef – in charge of the kitchen. In large establishments, the job title may be Executive Chef.
- Second Chef – directly in charge of food production.
- Pastry Chef – prepares pastries and desserts.
- Larder Chef – prepares cold foods, including salads, dressings, pâtés, cold hors d'oeuvres and buffet items.
- Sauce Chef – prepares sauces, stews and hot hors d'oeuvres; sautés food to order. This is usually the highest position of all the stations.

- Vegetable Chef – prepares vegetables, soups, starches and eggs.
- Assistant Chef – helps in all areas of the kitchen, generally doing the easier tasks.

Restaurant staff

Restaurant manager

The restaurant manager leads the team. They plan and implement the ways in which the staff work as a team. They are responsible for helping the staff acquire the skills needed and attitudes required for the job, including organising training for staff. They have overall responsibility for the smooth running of the restaurant and its future development. They organise rotas and inform staff of any changes to the menu or number of customers.

Waiting staff (waiters and waitresses)

The waiting staff work as part of a team. They advise customers about the menus and take their orders. They prepare and clear tables, serve customers and play an important role in customer care.

Risk assessment

The health and safety of the guests at an event is of prime importance.

A risk assessment must be carried out in order to:

- Identify the risks from all elements of the event
- Plan to minimise the risks
- Plan how to deal with problems if they occur.

A risk assessment should consider the following:

- HACCP (hazard analysis critical control points)
- Fire procedures
- Accident procedures
- First aid
- Hygiene regulations
- The Food Safety Act
- COSHH (control of substances hazardous to health)
- Health and Safety Executive (HSE) five-point plan.

 TERMINOLOGY:

Waiting staff: The waiters and waitresses are often referred to as 'waiting staff'.

Greeting and seating: How the customers are met and taken to their table.

Seating plan: A plan of who will be sitting where on what table.

COSTING MENUS AND EVENTS

When planning menus and events it is important to ensure that you cover the cost of the ingredients and allow for all your overheads, such as fuel and labour. Normally you should aim for between 40 per cent and 60 per cent profit. Think about what ingredients are available at the time of your event and ensure you are not choosing ingredients that are very expensive. If you decide to use commodities that are expensive you may decide to make smaller portions. (For example, salmon is expensive so you can serve smaller portions – customers know that this is an expensive item.) You should calculate the cost of the dish, including the trimmings and garnish, and ensure that you are charging more than the cost of the commodities if you are to make a profit.

Remember, if you are serving more than one dish you should work out the cost of all the food and then add your profit to work out the selling price.

Calculating the selling price

The 'selling price' of food is calculated (worked out) according to the amount of profit that an establishment wants to make. This is because the selling price has to take into account:

- the actual food cost (the cost of the ingredients)
- overheads (the cost of rates, gas, electricity, etc.)
- labour cost (staff wages)
- profit
- VAT.

The formula used in the catering industry to calculate selling price is:

> Food cost $\times$ 100 $\div$ 40

Example: If food costs were £4 the calculation would be:

> 4 (food cost) $\times$ 100 $\div$ 40 = 10

The selling price would be £10.

A simple way of calculating selling price is to multiply the food costs by 3.

Example: If food costs were £4 the calculation would be:

$$4 \times 3 = 12$$

The selling price would be £12.

Always remember to use the correct mathematical calculation. Some food costs are in £ and therefore involve a simple calculation. Some food costs are in pence, so you need to use a decimal point.

Sample calculations

If food costs were £2.50, the calculation would be:

$$2.50 \times 100 \div 40 = 6.25 \text{ (i.e. £6.25).}$$

If food costs were 60p the calculation would be:

$$60 \times 100 \div 40 = 1.50 \text{ (i.e. £1.50).}$$

VAT

Value Added Tax is a tax that is charged on all business to consumer transactions. For example, a hospitality outlet would charge VAT to a customer having a meal in a resturant.

VAT is added to all food and drink sold for consumption on the premises. Most take-away foods are also subject to VAT, depending on whether the foods are sold hot.

VAT currently stands at 15 per cent.

Why do we need customer care?

- Most hospitality and catering establishments rely on income from customers.
- Customers will be satisfied if their needs are met.
- Customers who are satisfied will come back.

To achieve good customer care you need to:

- put your customers first
- make them feel valued and important
- make them feel comfortable and safe
- make them want to return.

How customers enjoy their 'meal experience', whether in a fast-food outlet or high-class restaurant, depends on:

- the welcome or greeting they receive when they first arrive
- the décor - bright and colourful or warm with dim lights
- the atmosphere - lively or quiet
- the hygiene – the outlet needs to be clean and well presented (especially the toilets)
- the safety – fire exits need to be clearly marked
- the security – customers' belongings need to be safe
- the way customers' behave – if they are too noisy it may affect the enjoyment of others
- where the table is situated – quiet corner or centre of dining area
- the presentation of the menu and drinks list
- whether all menu items are available
- the speed, efficiency and quality of service
- polite and helpful staff
- attentive staff
- the quality of the food
- value for money
- how questions are answered
- how problems and complaints are handled
- how the bill is presented and payment taken
- how customers are treated when they leave.

Good customer care in a restaurant means staff doing their best to make sure customers enjoy their 'meal experience'.

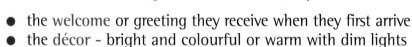

What are standards of customer care?

Imagine you are a customer visiting a restaurant for the first time. What are you looking for? What are you expecting?

Your answers are the 'standards' of customer care you expect.

They may include:

- a clean and well presented entrance
- a warm welcome from head waiter, restaurant manager or receptionist
- sample menu and drinks list are on display
- staff who are smartly dressed and well groomed
- staff who smile when they speak to customers
- customers are shown to their tables quickly
- if there is a delay, staff apologise and give a reason
- customers are served efficiently
- staff who are polite and attentive
- staff who are helpful
- staff who understand customers' needs
- staff who have a professional attitude
- staff who make each customer feel special
- staff who escort customers to the door at the end of the meal and say 'Have a good day' or 'Goodnight'.

Look at the picture below and say what you would need to do as restaurant manager to sort out the problems and keep customers happy.

The level of service

Technical skills and techniques are important in customer care, but even more important are sincere and caring attitudes and manners, which make customers feel at ease, welcome and wanted. Most establishments have their own 'customer care policy', which will set out the standards required and training policies.

If the level of service is

- attentive and efficient – but not rushed
- friendly and welcoming – but not too familiar
- helpful – when advising on dishes and drinks

then the expectations of most customers will be met. It does not matter whether the service is self-service or waited service. Customers' expectations are based on the **level** of service and not the **type** of service.

Measuring customer care

Monitoring customer feedback helps organisations provide more effective customer care. Feedback from customers can be formal (written) or informal (verbal or by obervation).

Comment cards and questionnaires are the most common ways of obtaining feedback.

- Comment cards are short and give a fairly 'instant' feedback. They are designed to be brief and often require a 'yes' or a 'no' answer or a tick box rating.
- Questionnaires are often used as a means of getting more detailed information. They often include a range of questions that need customers to express opinions or feelings. Sometimes customers are offered incentives, such as being entered in a prize draw, to answer questionnaires.

Informal feedback is also useful and comes from:

- Talking to customers – asking if they have enjoyed their meal, etc.
- Observing customers – unhappy customers can show dissatisfaction by their use of body language. Examples include frowning, tapping fingers on table, holding drinks up to the light, etc.

- Using mystery customers – the hospitality industry employs people who visit and stay in establishments and give an anonymous assessment of the service they are given.
- Using staff feedback – members of staff can provide good feedback about any standards of service they find difficult to meet and also suggest ideas for improving service.

REMEMBER

Remember the longer you leave an unhappy customer, the harder it will be to resolve the problem.

Problem-solving

Problems occur in the hospitality and catering industry all the time. Often there are *immediate* solutions to a problem but some problems need a more *long-term* solution.

Here are two examples:

1. The soup is cold.
   Immediate response: apologise, take back to kitchen, replace or offer alternative.
   Long-term response: refer to head chef to make sure correct training and checking procedures are in place.
2. A tap is dripping in a hotel bedroom.
   Immediate response: Send maintenance to fix problem. This will prevent accidents, water damage and loss of water.
   Long-term response: Regular checking, reporting, maintenance and repair.

Dealing with problems and complaints becomes easier with practice but there are 'set' procedures to follow. It is useful to practise these procedures in a 'safe' environment, such as a school restaurant, or by doing role-plays within your group. This will help to build your confidence.

Every establishment will have its own rules and regulations. What you are allowed to do will depend upon your position or level of responsibility. For example, you would not be allowed to offer a discount or vouchers to a customer who complains if you had just started a job as a waiter in a local restaurant – you would need to ask your supervisor to deal with the situation.

Typical complaints procedure

If a customer complains about the food or service in the restaurant you should:

- Stay calm. Listen attentively to what the customer has to say (some customers find it difficult to complain, so once they start they do not want to be interrupted!).
- Apologise.
- Try to resolve the situation. For example, if the food is cold or not up to standard in some other way, take it back to the kitchen and report it to the head chef and the restaurant manager. Offer the customer a replacement or an alternative dish.
- Explain to the customer what you intend to do (e.g. bring their replacement dish within five minutes, if they have agreed that this is acceptable, or ask the restaurant manager to deal with their concerns).
- Apologise again for the problem.

Handling compliments

Sometimes you will receive compliments, especially if you give good service or if customers enjoy the meal you serve. Some staff find this just as difficult to deal with as complaints.

When you receive a compliment you should do the following:

- Thank the customer for their comments and show you are pleased to receive the compliment.
- Ask if you could do anything to improve next time!
- Pass on compliments to others, especially to the chefs if the compliments are about the food.

Corporate image

Some companies within the hospitality and catering industry have their own corporate image, e.g. Forté Hotels and fast food outlets such as McDonalds.

They are easily identifiable by:

- logo
- uniform/dress code
- menu
- layout of establishment
- advertising.

! **REMEMBER**

Remember that you may not have the authority to offer free drinks, money off the bill or vouchers, so seek the help of someone who has.

Logos are used to encourage customers to recognise the establishment: they will be aware of the brand and may feel comfortable as they know what to expect from the company. Logos are used across all establishments within the company.

Uniform/dress code: some companies insist that all staff wear the same uniform; this makes them easily identifiable for staff and customers. It saves staff paying for uniforms and they are often laundered by the company. The uniform may change depending on which area of the establishment they work in.

Menu: often the menu chosen in large companies is the same no matter where you are in the country or abroad, e.g McDonalds, Brewster's Fayre or Beefeater. This enables the companies to arrange large orders with manufacturers and possibly to make big savings and therefore more profit. Customers get to know the menu and are familiar with it.

Layout of the establishment can be the same or similar across the country: this makes the customers feel secure and at home no matter where they are, e.g. Little Chef, McDonalds and Burger King. Again the customer knows what to expect in each of these.

Advertising: large international companies spend millions on advertising and promoting their products and services. Many companies combine with others to run joint promotional activities; for example, Virgin Atlantic offer special discount deals on car hire and hotel accommodation when purchasing an airline ticket; McDonalds has links with Disney and gives away 'free' children's toys when new films are released.

It is important that you understand about standards of service and how to make sure that staff are providing reliable services to customers.

You should be able to identify acceptable service standards in the following working areas:

- reception, front-of-house, food service
- meeting, greeting and bidding farewell
- responding to enquiries
- dealing with complaints
- presenting bills.

Customers like to feel welcome and important when they visit any establishment. The first members of staff they encounter are reception or front-of-house, so it is important that the staff are friendly and approachable. If there is a queue, try to acknowledge that you are aware that people are waiting and tell them you won't be long. When you are able to deal with the customer, apologise for the wait. When customers leave, say 'thank you' and 'goodbye'. Remember that 'manners are free' and they go a long way to making the customer happy and satisfied with the service they have received.

TERMINOLOGY:

Complaint: expression of dissatisfaction.

Response: how you react verbally and in your body language.

Review: look back on something to see how it was dealt with.

ACTIVITY

Try to find out:

- how customers are greeted at reception
- how complaints are handled
- how customers are approached for their orders in the restaurant and bar
- if staff are friendly and helpful
- the 'extras' that are provided with the coffee in conference rooms.

When you are recording your information, try to include an incident that happened on your placement. Describe how it was dealt with and how the customer felt afterwards. Do you think the incident was dealt with correctly? What would you have done?

Standards of service link with customer care, the next area we look at. Customer care is a major aspect of the industry. Most establishments have standards that must be met by all staff. Reviews and training take place regularly.

Customer care

In this section of your work you should include information on the importance of good customer care. You should be able to identify, apply and evaluate customer care effectively. Customer care is not just about talking to the customers when there is a problem. The following also need to be considered:

- attitude
- appearance
- manner
- body language
- voice.

We have all seen or heard about incidents of poor customer care. Perhaps you have been on the receiving end yourself. Let's look at a scenario of events. See how many things you identify as good and poor customer care.

Bob and Sue have pre-booked a hotel close to an event they are going to see on a Sunday. They set off to the hotel on the Saturday afternoon. Half way there, they receive a call from the hotel stating that there is a problem with the room. The hotel staff tell Bob and Sue that they have arranged for them to stay in another hotel close to the event. Bob and Sue feel that this is acceptable and thank the hotel for letting them know.

They arrive at the new hotel at around 4 pm. On arrival they explain to the staff what has happened. The receptionist tells them the other hotel had double booked, as the event was so popular. Bob is a little annoyed about this, but does not say anything. He then asks what time they could have their evening meal. He is told to ask the manager, who is near the bar. The manager says they are very busy with a carvery buffet at six, but they can eat around half past six. Bob thanks the manager and goes to find the room.

At half past six, Bob and Sue make their way to the dining room. It is very busy, so they check it is still alright to eat there. The manager tells them to take a seat and that someone will be with them shortly. At half past seven, they are still waiting for their order to be taken. The group having the carvery are still being served and another group are waiting to come in. Bob goes to speak to the manager again. He is told that someone will be along to take their order and the manager apologises for the inconvenience. At eight they are still waiting, so Sue goes to speak to the manager. The manager says he is very sorry but they have two carvery buffets booked and it is the first time they have done an event like this. He sends one of the waitresses to take their order straight away and offers them a free bottle of wine. They eventually get their meal at nine o clock, at no charge.

ACTIVITY

There are examples of both good and bad customer care in this scenario. Identify these as a group and discuss what you think should have happened.

When you are thinking about customer care, you should also take into account the way in which the staff respond to the customer. It is important to show good manners toward the customer. Your appearance also goes a long way, as does your body language.

If a customer has a complaint you should:

● apologise
● tell them you will deal with the complaint
● take their name and room number or address
● pass on the information to your supervisor or manager
● go back and let the customer know it is being dealt with.

REMEMBER

Remember that your supervisor or manager will notice your appearance and body language. It will not look good if you respond to the customer by saying, 'Yeah, so what do you want me to do about it?' while slouching with your hands in your pockets and chewing gum.

The supervisor or manager should then:

● find out the details
● speak to the member of staff concerned
● explain to the customer what has happened
● offer some form of compensation
● apologise to the customer again
● offer additional training to the staff on customer care.

ACTIVITY

Role-play:

- In small groups, think about something that a customer might complain about.
- Act out the event, showing poor customer care.
- Discuss the role-play with the rest of the class.
- Act out the role-play again, this time showing good customer care.
- Record your thoughts in your book.

TERMINOLOGY:

Attitude: The way in which you approach customers.

Appearance: The way you look to customers. It is important to look clean and smart.

Manner: The way you speak to customers.

Body language: The way in which your body reflects your mood.

Voice: The tone of voice you use to customers.

Quality assurance and quality control are systems that are used within the hospitality and catering industry to ensure that customers have products and services that are of a consistent standard.

The best-known quality assurance systems are produced by the national tourist organisations for Britain (namely Visit Britain, Visit Wales and Visit Scotland) and the AA, where stars are awarded to establishments to show the quality of facilities and service they offer.

Restaurants are also involved in star ratings. Michelin stars are awarded every year to those providing an excellent standard of food and restaurants that are rated 'very good' or better feature *The Good Food Guide*.

How do we judge quality?

The quality of a product or service can be difficult to define because it is determined (decided upon) by the customer's own perception (understanding or experience).

Products and services

When judging the quality of a product (such as a meal served in a restaurant), there are fewer variables to consider. Are the dishes beautifully cooked and presented, the correct consistency, well-seasoned? If the answer to all of these is 'yes', then the quality can be said to be good.

However, with a service (such as the serving of a meal in a restaurant), quality is more difficult to define. Research has found that customers judge the quality of service in many different ways. These are outlined below.

Reliability

Carrying out the service at the expected or appropriate time. This means that guests are not kept waiting. Hotel bills should be accurate so that guests do not have to question or challenge them. Accurate records are kept for any queries.

A beautifully presented tomato salad

Responding quickly to customers

Members of staff deal with customers willingly and promptly.

Competence

Members of staff have the skills and knowledge to carry out the service.

Accessibility

Members of staff are easily accessible. no matter what time of day or night it is. Staff are also approachable and friendly.

Courtesy

Members of staff are polite, considerate and friendly without being 'familiar'. Staff are also well-groomed and show respect to customers and their property.

Credibility

Members of staff are trustworthy and honest. Staff have the customers' well-being and enjoyment as their first concern.

Communication

Members of staff should be able to cater for different customers' needs – this may involve addressing the customers in their language, or simply by being clear and concise when dealing with problems and queries. Customers need to know that problems will be handled quickly and effectively.

Security

Customers need to be assured of their physical safety (to be free from danger or risk), to have financial security (e.g. their bank details secure) and confidentiality (other people should not have access to confidential information about them).

Meeting customer needs

Members of staff find out what the customer needs are, and meet or exceed these needs with good customer care. Staff should recognise 'regular' customers and make them feel welcome.

Other factors

Other factors that contribute to quality include the surroundings, the appearance of staff and the tools or equipment used to provide the service (this could be the plates used in a restaurant).

Quality will also be affected by other customers. If other customers are noisy or disorderly, it will affect people's enjoyment of a meal or their stay in a hotel.

Sometimes customers make up their minds about the quality of service they expect *before* they receive that service.

REMEMBER

Remember that service quality can be:
- Poor = does not meet expectations.
- Normal = as expected.
- Exceptional = exceeds expectations.

ACTIVITY

Imagine that you are going to McDonald's with a group of friends to buy a burger. What are you expecting of the service?

Imagine you are going to a wedding reception which is to be held in a four-star hotel. What are you expecting of the service?

Is it easy to imagine the different standards you would expect?

Accommodation ratings

The national tourism agency 'Visit Britain' is responsible for marketing Britain worldwide and for developing Britain's visitor economy. It has created new rating standards for accommodation. This includes hotels and guest accommodation, using stars to represent hotels and diamonds for guest accommodation, including guest houses, inns, farmhouses and bed-and-breakfast establishments. Self-catering accommodation and caravan parks are also represented by stars under the new system.

What to expect with each star rating

Five-star luxury hotels

These offer first-class services and accommodation with elegant and luxurious surroundings. The hotel restaurants often have famous chefs with a high standard of cuisine. Hotels are usually situated in desirable locations in major cities and resorts. Facilities include valet parking, concierge service, room service, well-equipped fitness centres and modern business centres.

Four-star deluxe hotels

These offer a comfort, class and quality that customers can rely on. The hotel will usually be situated in a prime location near to desirable shops and restaurants. Facilities may include valet parking, concierge service, room service, well equipped fitness centres and business centres.

Three-star mid-scale hotels

These are often situated near motorways, in city centres and suburbs. Rooms and reception areas are nicely furnished and offer a degree of comfort. Facilities may include swimming pools, fitness centres, room service and parking. There are restaurants within the hotels.

Two-star value hotels

These are often situated near office parks, airports, shopping and retail areas. Rooms are comfortably decorated but not elegant. Usually these hotels do not have

restaurants or room service but offer free parking and sometimes a swimming pool. Transport may be available to nearby airports.

One-star economy hotels and motels

These are often situated near major motorways. They offer simple, basic accommodation. Facilities include free parking, cable TV and tea- and coffee-making facilities in the rooms. Restaurants are often located nearby and room service is not available. Some economy hotels and motels have swimming pools.

What to expect with each diamond rating

Five-diamond

These offer an excellent overall quality with plenty of space, high-quality furniture and excellent interior design. Breakfasts are fresh and often use seasonal, local ingredients when possible. There are excellent levels of customer care, anticipating customers' every need.

Four-diamond

These offer a very good overall level of quality, including comfortable bedrooms and a well maintained décor. Breakfasts offer a good choice of quality items, freshly cooked. There are very good levels of customer care, showing attention to customers' needs.

Three-diamond

These offer a good overall level of quality, including comfortable bedrooms and a well maintained, practical décor. Breakfasts offer a good choice of quality items, freshly cooked. There is a good level of comfort with good levels of customer care.

Two-diamond

These offer clean, comfortable accommodation with functional décor. Breakfasts may be continental or cooked. There is a sound level of quality and customer care in all areas.

A bedroom in a two-diamond hotel

One-diamond

These offer clean accommodation with an acceptable level of comfort and functional décor. Breakfasts may be continental or cooked. There is an acceptable level of quality and helpful service.

Self-catering

Properties have to provide the following before they can be considered for a star rating:

- a high standard of cleanliness throughout
- the prices and conditions of booking made clear
- local information provided so that customers make the most of their stay
- comfortable accommodation with a range of furniture to meet customer needs
- colour TV at no extra charge
- kitchen equipment to meet essential needs.

The more stars, the higher the overall quality. Once properties have met the minimum requirements, increased levels of quality then apply. Customers will find an acceptable level of quality at one-star, very good quality at three-star and exceptional quality at five-star.

Caravan parks

The star rating for caravan parks has been designed to reflect the quality and facilities that customers expect in caravan parks. A rating from one to five stars is awarded, based on cleanliness, environment and the quality of the facilities and service offered:

- one star - acceptable quality.
- two stars - good quality.
- three stars - very good quality.
- four stars - excellent quality.
- five stars - exceptional quality.

Accessibility

Not every customer has full mobility. Visit Britain's National Accessible Scheme places establishments in different categories of accessibility:

1. Accessible to someone who can climb a flight of stairs but would benefit from fixtures and fittings to aid balance.
2. Accessible to someone with restricted walking ability who is able to walk up a maximum of three steps.
3. Accessible to someone who depends on a wheelchair but transfers to and from the wheelchair unaided.
4. Accessible to someone who depends on a wheelchair and needs assistance.
5. Exceptional access for independent wheelchair users.
6. Exceptional access for independent wheelchair users and those who need assistance.

Establishments that have been rated will display National Accessible Scheme symbols.

Modern trends in planning and design mean that many restaurants have their kitchen areas in view. In the same way, modern hotels have the different areas of the hotel close together, so that they are easily accessible for customers and staff, and also save money and fuel.

The different areas

The entrance

A guest's experience of staying in a hotel starts at the entrance. The grounds and entrance provide important clues as to the type of hotel it is, so these need to reflect the style of the interior.

ACTIVITY

Look at the entrances to these hotels – do they all look like hotels?

Explain why they do, or do not.

What would your expectations of each hotel be?

Clues: Hotels may be budget, luxurious, traditional, and either commercial (i.e. for the business traveller) or for leisure.

Reception areas

The reception area of a hotel is often said to be the 'nerve centre' of the hotel. It is the first contact point with the customer and often the last. The saying 'you only have one chance to make a first impression' is especially true of the reception area and staff. The reception desk needs to be seen clearly from the entrance. To improve security, the desk should be positioned so that staff can keep an eye on the whole area.

Factors that influence reception design include:

- the size of the hotel
- the number of staff
- the need for security
- the décor/image required, e.g. hotel groups often have recognisable features which are the same in every hotel
- the space available – customers often wait in reception areas for friends to arrive, taxis to collect them, etc.
- the need for a large enough reception area to deal with the volume of customers that book in at any one time
- access for computer terminal points
- the need to be warm and welcoming
- the level of comfort needed – the higher the star rating the higher the level of comfort provided
- the type of customer who uses the hotel
- well-signed access to bedrooms, the restaurant and other areas of the hotel.

Accommodation areas

Bedrooms in hotels may vary in style, but generally they are very similar. Guests require a bed, somewhere to hang or store their clothes, a bedside cabinet and some form of luggage storage. If bedrooms have en-suite bathrooms, these should contain a toilet, a hand basin, a shower and/or bath.

Designs of bedrooms can vary from fun to vivid, colourful to brash and unique to quaint. Some rural (country) hotels like to create the atmosphere of a luxury country house to attract foreign visitors. Some city centre hotels ensure guests have all the facilities they need to carry on their business from their hotel room.

Factors that influence the design of accommodation areas include:

- the type of hotel (budget, luxurious, traditional, commercial (for the business guest), a leisure centre, etc.)
- corporate identity – an identical design may be used by every hotel in a particular chain
- the level of comfort needed
- the level of facilities and services needed.

Restaurant areas

Hotel guests do not always want a large meal in a formal restaurant. Larger hotels may have several restaurants that vary in level of formality and the type and price of menu offered. Some hotels have bars serving coffee and light snacks. These offer a good alternative to full meals and can also be used to attract non-residents to the hotel.

The interior design of a restaurant (i.e. the colours and finishes, the furnishings, the lighting and layout) all work together to create a particular atmosphere. Guests often like to eat in interesting and different surroundings. Large hotels often give their restaurants a distinctive flavour or theme. The more unusual a restaurant is, the more likely guests are to tell their friends about it.

Breakfast in a hotel restaurant

Factors that influence the design of the restaurant/eating areas include:

- the sort of menu that is on offer
- the sort of service that is needed – self service or waited service
- how the food and drink is displayed or served
- the facilities (food display counter, bar area, etc.) that will be needed
- how many staff will be needed.

Kitchen areas

Before a kitchen is planned, several factors need to be considered, including the type of customer, the menu and style of food service. Kitchens should be designed so that they are easy to manage in terms of efficiency and hygiene. It is a good idea to have a flow of work through the kitchen, from delivery – storage – prep – cooking – chilling – hot-holding – serving – washing up – refuse disposal.

Factors that influence kitchen design include:

- the amount of money available to spend
- whether the kitchen is 'new-build' or a refit
- the space available
- the size of the food service area and number of covers needed
- the style of food service (e.g. a carvery service has different needs to fast-food service)

- the proximity (nearness) of the food service area
- services available – gas, electricity and water
- staff skills
- the menu to be offered – using pre-prepared meals or a lot of convenience foods will require fewer staff and less equipment
- the equipment available
- where equipment is situated (large items of equipment already 'in situ' may be impossible to move)
- storage areas
- legislation – kitchens must conform to Food Hygiene Regulations, the Food Safety Act, etc.

Multi-usage requirements

Some establishments, such as hospitals and factories, have peak times when the whole of the kitchen area needs to be used. They also have quiet times when only a small number of people require food and drink. Modern kitchens are planned to be more adaptable, so that whole sections can be closed down when not in use. This means that unused sections do not need heating or lighting. Multi-use kitchens therefore save money and are kinder to the environment.

In the hospitality and catering industry, it is usual to work as a member of a team. This might be in the kitchen (as one of the kitchen brigade), in the restaurant (as one of the restaurant brigade), in the accommodation operations or front-of-house. Sometimes teams are called groups. Every member of staff needs to feel part of a group or team. The hospitality and catering industry relies heavily on 'teamwork' to provide the products and services the customer wants.

How do teams work?

In an organised team such as the kitchen brigade, every member of the team has a responsibility in the production of food. Each kitchen brigade will have a definite structure and set procedures. The team leader (i.e. the head chef) will:

- decide who works in the team
- decide what the team has to do
- take responsibility for the standard of work produced
- make sure that current legislation standards are met.

Stages in teamwork

Teams go through several stages before they are able to achieve excellent standards.

Stage 1

The team is given a task. Each person in the team has to understand what the task is and the best way of achieving a good end result.

Example: Your team/group has been asked to plan a menu for the retirement party for your head teacher. What other information will you need before deciding on the menu?

Stage 2

The team goes through a stage of 'disagreement' when different ideas are put forward and discussed.

Example: Your team/group cannot decide whether to have a buffet or a sit-down meal for the party.

Stage 3

The team starts to work together as one unit, instead of one person trying to dominate the others or get all their ideas chosen.

Example: Your team/group decides to accept a majority decision and then everyone works together to plan the best menu.

Stage 4

The team works very well together.

Example: Your team/group plans a buffet menu that will suit all dietary needs.

How can you recognise good teamwork?

- Team members communicate (talk to each other) effectively.
- Team members feel able to suggest ideas.
- Team members know what is expected of them.
- Team members 'share' responsibility to make sure that tasks are done.
- Tasks are carried out quickly.
- Tasks are carried out effectively.
- Team members are happy in their jobs.
- Team members have high self-esteem.

What affects team behaviour?

- Strong personalities that want to dominate.
- Individual characteristics, i.e. qualities of team members.
- Cultural differences.
- Social skills of team members.
- Conflicts or personality clashes within the team.
- Pressure.
- Stress.
- Change, e.g. in home circumstances or working practices.
- Attitude and behaviour of the team leader.

How can you recognise good team leaders?

Team leaders or supervisors often have very good technical skills, knowledge and ability. Good team leaders should be able to:

- delegate tasks effectively
- motivate their teams
- communicate effectively
- give advice, support and training
- help team members to develop performance
- maintain quality
- monitor the work of team members
- give praise
- recognise individual contribution to the team
- give constructive and positive feedback
- check the team is meeting its objectives – whether it is meeting financial targets or gaining a Michelin star!

Managing your team

To have an effective team in the hospitality industry, you need a good team leader. Good communication is the key to success.

Planning and prioritising

- Keep everyone in the team fully informed of any plans.
- Let team members contribute their ideas to the team leader.
- Make sure team members' roles and responsibilities are clear.
- Prioritise objectives.
- Be aware of the 'whole' picture – oversee work throughout the day.
- Update plans regularly.

Monitoring and giving feedback

- Provide the staff with a sense of achievement – praise often.
- Be clear and use agreed criteria when giving feedback.
- Choose a suitable time and place to give feedback.
- Begin with positive feedback, then deal with underlying issues.
- Let team members respond.
- Keep written records clear.
- Share all outcomes.

Problem-solving and decision-making

- Be welcoming, relaxed and confident when dealing with problems.
- Create open forums or team meetings to discuss issues in the open – this boosts staff morale.
- Minimise conflict by finding 'common ground'.
- Anticipate and avert problems.
- Get to the root of problems quickly.

Motivating and developing staff

- Make staff responsible for their own training, but support them fully.
- Set clear targets.
- Motivate with enthusiasm, giving help, giving encouragement and leading by example.
- Reward good work.

Communication

- Listen to your staff.
- Express yourself clearly.
- Check understanding.

Target setting

- Win the loyalty of your staff and customers by setting challenging yet achievable goals/targets.
- Focus on results.
- Make sure you do your best in *your* work.

ACTIVITY

Look at the descriptions above and think about if you have the qualities to become a good team leader. Or are you more of a team player? Why do you think this is? What skills do you need to develop to become a good team leader or team player? Note down your thoughts.

Communication

You need to understand the importance of effective communication in the following:

- Administrative procedures, e.g. filing, processing, enquiries
- Billing of customers – methods of payments
- Booking systems – procedures and recording
- Customer care – welcome, body language, meeting databases, word processing, email
- ICT skills, e.g. databases, word processing, email
- Storage of personal data – governed by the Data Protection Act.

Administrative procedures

Front office departments carry out many of the administration tasks required in the hospitality industry. Front office consists of reception, reservations, administration, guest services and porters. The work covers:

- reservations
- dealing with amendments, cancellations and enquiries
- communicating with other departments, e.g. housekeeping
- security, e.g. dealing with lost property, issue of keys, etc.
- check in
- registration
- guest accounting
- check out
- guest services, e.g. concierge, porters
- administration, e.g. filing, updating guest records, etc.
- customer care
- answering the telephone.

Billing of customers

This can be very complex. When guests book into a hotel they start to acquire charges on their account, for example, through the bar, restaurant, room service, in-house movies, leisure facilities, etc. In a large hotel, each department notes these changes and this information is sent to the front office. Front office staff are responsible for placing all charges onto a guest's bill. In most hotels this is carried out by computer – the charges are sent to front office via the various points of sale (POS). In small hotels, the charges must be recorded and carried manually to the front desk. Accuracy is essential in any guest billing or accounting system so that up-to-date records for every guest are maintained. Guest billing also provides each department of the hotel with accurate financial information.

Booking systems

Bookings may be taken by post, email, telephone, via the Internet and in person. A booking is very often the first contact that a guest has with an establishment so it is important to create the right impression. Most establishments use some form of booking sheet, which can be manual or electronic. Bookings can be taken for accommodation, a table in a restaurant, a wedding reception, etc.

When taking a booking some essential information is needed:

- guest's name and telephone number
- the day and date the booking is needed
- the number of rooms/covers
- the time the booking is needed
- any special requests.

It is a good idea for the person taking the booking to repeat the information back to the guest for confirmation that all the details are correct. Some guests may want written confirmation of their booking, particularly if the booking request was received by post or email.

Customer care

Front office staff play a vital role in customer care because they are the first people guests see when they book in.

Staff appearance and the welcome guests receive when entering an establishment will determine a guest's 'first impression' of that establishment. Good customer care is vital because it:

- benefits the guests, as they feel welcomed and cared for
- benefits the organisation, as it leads to repeat business and therefore more profit
- benefits the staff, as it leads to higher self-esteem and greater job satisfaction.

ICT skills

ICT skills are increasingly important because of the advances in computer technology. It does not matter how simple or advanced the computer system is, it will not be effective if the person using the system does not understand it or cannot operate it successfully.

Front office staff are often trained to use a particular reservation system that operates in the hotel where they are employed, e.g. Fidelio. All front office staff need:

- good literacy skills, e.g. accurate spelling
- good communication skills for letter writing
- good word-processing skills
- accuracy when entering data on a database
- a good understanding of different programs and software packages.

Storage of personal data

The Data Protection Act 1998 requires all organisations that hold data about individuals on computerised systems to register with the Data Protection Registrar. Examples in hospitality include guest reservation systems, guest registration forms, guest history files, mailing lists, etc. The Act gives customers the right to

- be informed of **where** the data is being processed
- have a **description** of all the details being held
- know **why** the data is being held
- know **who** has access to it.

Front office staff must be aware of their responsibilities under the Data Protection Act because they are primarily responsible for guests' security.

Within the hospitality industry it is important that we take into account environmental issues. You should have an understanding of how to conserve energy and water, reduce, reuse and recycling of waste from establishments and understand why it is important for the industry to address these areas.

Conservation of energy and water

There are many ways in which the hospitality industry can conserve water and encourage their guests to do the same. Below are some examples:

- Use towels more than once – many hotels now have signs in the bathrooms to encourage guests to use the towels again by hanging them back up, this reduces the amount of times they are washed therefore saving water.
- Fit showers rather than baths – showering uses less water than baths.
- Having taps that only send out short bursts of water when customers are washing their hands.
- Using washing up water to water the gardens, or having a water butt to catch rainwater.
- Only serving water on the tables when the guests ask for it.

Hospitality establishments can also save energy by:

- having lights that work only when the key card is placed in the slot
- setting the heating to come on for a few hours a day or only when the guest is in the room
- having air conditioning on only when the guest is in the room
- advising the guests of the establishment's policy on helping the environment and asking them to unplug electrical equipment when not in use and not to leave equipment such as computers on standby
- using energy saving light bulbs
- thermostatically setting hot water and heating
- installing modern toilets that use less flush water.

At Anglia World Hotels, we know that many of our customers are concerned about protecting the environment. To reduce the amount of water and detergent that we use, we will not remove all towels for cleaning every day during your stay. If you would like your towels to be replaced today, please leave them in the bath.

Reduce, reuse, recycle

Hospitality establishments can reduce, reuse and recycle the waste they produce by:

Reduce

Recycle   Reuse

- only issuing newspapers when the guest requests them
- fitting large shower soaps to the wall that can be refilled rather than using individual bottles
- reusing paper for notes and messages
- not printing out information if they don't need to, pass on information by email
- buying ingredients that are fresh or in less packaging
- buying ingredients in bulk
- reusing large containers to store things in
- encouraging guests to recycle by putting recycle bins around the building
- recycling glass, tins, cardboard and paper
- cutting down on the number of free items given to guests in their bedrooms, for example sewing kits and slippers
- sending food waste to local farms for animal feed
- using vegetable peelings to make a compost for the garden
- not putting new toilet rolls out for new guests, but making the remaining half of the roll look good by folding the edges in to a peak.

It is important for the hospitality industry to act now and encourage guests to save the environment as it gives the industry a good reputation and allows the guests to see that they care about what is happening to the world. Setting a good example encourages others to do the same.

REMEMBER

Remember the three Rs: reduce, reuse, recycle.

CHAPTER 4

ASSESSMENT FOR GCSE HOSPITALITY (SINGLE AWARD)

4.1 CONTROLLED ASSESSMENT: EVENT BASED TASK

Unit 3 is assessed through a folio of evidence for an event that you have carried out. Your folio is worth 60 per cent of your final grade for the single award in Hospitality or 30 per cent of the Double Award in Hospitality and Catering. You should include the following sections:

- Investigating the task – 20 marks
- Planning the task – 15 marks
- Carrying out the task – 60 marks
- Evaluating the task – 25 marks.

Examples of events you could run

You should plan and hold an event from one of the following criteria.

- Many charities rely on fundraising events. Research, plan and carry out a fundraising event.
- Celebrations of all kinds are often large events. Research, plan and carry out a celebratory event.
- Schools and colleges host many events during the year. Research, plan and carry out such an event.

Your event must cater for **at least ten people**. Let's look at some examples of events with brief descriptions.

Fundraising events

Pizza café

Work as a group to make a selection of pizzas to be sold at lunch time to pupils and staff. The pizzas would be portioned and sold by the slice. Profit made will be given to a charity, e.g. Children in Need.

Coffee shop

You are allocated a sum of money. You will decide what to make and sell to pupils and staff. Your event could take place at breaktime or lunchtime.

Celebration events

Senior citizens' tea

Plan and hold an afternoon tea for a group of senior citizens. Link with the drama department and get them to organise entertainment.

Prize-giving

Prepare, cook and serve food at the prize-giving event in school. This could be a buffet suitable for all dietary needs.

School events

Three-course meal for staff

Prepare, cook and serve a three-course meal for a selected number of staff, for example senior staff and governors.

Gourmet meal for parents and staff

Link with your local college of further education and use their training restaurant and kitchens to prepare and serve a gourmet meal for parents and staff.

ACTIVITY

Think of other ideas of events you could hold in each of the categories. Remember that your event must cater for a minimum of ten people.

So how do you ensure you get maximum marks for your event? Let's look at each section again and see how the marks are awarded.

Investigating the task (20 marks)

You should include information under the following headings in your investigation:

- Exploring themes and events. Look at a range of events that you could complete and show this work in your evidence. This could be in the form of a 'thought shower' or 'mood board'. Give reasons for the choices you have made.

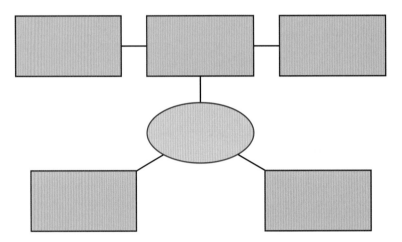

- Venues and seating arrangements. Look at areas around your school or college and see which ones are suitable and why. List the pros and cons of holding the event there. You may wish to add photographs to illustrate reasons why they are/are not suitable.
- Show how you will set up the area for the event. Look at different table layouts and decide which one is best for the type of event you are holding. Again, give reasons for your choice.
- Staff – roles and responsibilities. Within your team, look at the job roles you will need to include when holding a successful event. Decide who will take on these roles and describe their responsibilities on the day. It is fine to share the workload for the event, as this is what happens in the industry.
- Resources. What equipment do you need to hold the event? Do you have that equipment in school, or will you have to hire it or borrow it? How much time have you got to prepare for the event? Include a weekly breakdown of what needs to be completed and when. It is a good idea to have another column where you say if the work has been completed so you can keep track of what still needs to be done. Look at the following example.

Weekly breakdown of work

Week/ Date	Theory work	Practical work	Work completed
1	Thought shower of ideas Decide on event Look at venues	Practical trial of food that could be made for the event	
2	Staff roles Resources needed Examples of dishes Type of customer	Second dish for event	

- Cost. You will need to look at how much the event is going to cost to run and the cost of the ingredients, equipment and sundries (extras like clingfilm, foil, disposable napkins, etc.). From this you will then be able to work out how much you will charge for people to attend the event. Remember that you should aim to make at least 40 per cent profit.
- Dishes/menu. Think about the type of dishes you can serve for your event. This could be a thought shower or mood board of ideas. Remember to think of a range of dishes and include special dietary needs. When you have decided in your team you should produce a menu for the event. You will need to look at the range of menus available and decide which one is most suitable for your event.

In order for you to access the higher range of marks for this section you should:

- produce a record of your research
- select and interpret the information to show you have knowledge of the event with realistic time scales identified
- write in a clear and well structured way
- show a good use of specialist vocabulary
- analyse your research.

Planning the task (15 marks)

When planning the task it is important to include the following:

Example of a risk assessment chart

Hazard	Who might be harmed?	Is the risk adequately controlled?	Further action required to control risk
Special dietary requirements	Customers	Staff have checked dietary requirements	Check that meals are OK before they are eaten
Fire	All	Fire procedure checked	Fire procedure gone over with pupils
Hazards relating to group activities, including cuts and burns	All	All safety procedures gone over with pupils	First aid kit carried Pupils briefed on safety before taking part in activities
Accidental falls	All	Tables set out with clear access No obstructions on the floor	Check that all areas of the floor are clear No table cloths hanging down to the floor

- Risk assessment chart. This should show all the accidents that could happen, who could be harmed and what you will do to prevent the accident. You could also include an HACCP chart for one of the high-risk foods you are producing. Remember to include fire safety in your risk assessment.

- Group/individual plan. This should be a time plan for the day of the event. It is a good idea to include everyone's jobs on the day, so that if someone is absent you will know what that person should have been doing and who can fill in their role for the day. You should include times, jobs and who is responsible for the job.

- Venue. Show how the venue will be set out for the event and how the tables will be laid. You could also include a room plan for the kitchen area, showing what foods will be made where.

- Dishes/menu. You should include recipes and photographs of the products that you have trialled during the planning stages. Include reasons why the dishes are suitable for the event.

- Costing/quantities/equipment. Ensure that you have included an accurate costing of the event and that you know how many portions each dish will serve. Remember to have spares in case of accidents. It is a good idea to write an equipment list to ensure you have sufficient equipment to hold a successful event.

Example of an HACCP chart for a product made in a school or college

Quality check	Process	Hygiene risk
Check quality	Store food in fridge △CCP	Bacterial growth
Check equipment not damaged	Collect equipment and ingredients Personal hygiene	Bacterial growth Staphylococcus aureus or E.coli
Check date	Prepare and chop protein food (meat or chicken) on a red board △CCP	Cross-contamination
Check freshness of vegetables	Prepare and chop vegetables on a green board	Cross-contamination Campylobacter from dirty vegetables
Not too much oil Visual check on meat changing colour	Put a little oil in the frying pan Add protein and cook until it seals	Salmonella from uncooked meat or poultry
Visual check on amount of sauce	Add vegetables and sauce	
Check more than one piece	Check core temperature of meat is at least 75°C	
Check wraps for consistency in size and shape	Prepare wrap Add salad	Campylobacter from soil on salad
Equal amount of filling in each Visual check for presentation	Add protein food and vegetables with sauce Serve while hot △CCP	Bacterial growth if food is not served immediately

- Theme/presentation. Will you have a theme for the event? How will the food be presented? Photographic evidence is good and can be used on the day to ensure that all the dishes look the same.
- Marketing. How have you advertised your event to your customers? Include examples of posters, invitations or tickets.

In order for you to access the higher range of marks for this section you should:

- produce a detailed/sequential plan
- ensure the plan supports the event fully
- explore a range of procedures necessary for the effective planning of the event
- communicate the information clearly in writing, with few errors
- use specialist vocabulary in your written work.

Carrying out the task (60 marks)

When carrying out the task you should consider the following:

- Personal presentation. You should be dressed correctly, showing that you can work safely and hygienically at all times. If possible, wear a hat and always wear an apron when preparing food.
- Safe practices/risk assessment (including hygiene). Photographic evidence should show that you are working safely at all times and using the correct equipment, e.g. the correct chopping boards to prevent cross contamination. Store your food safely and cover cuts with blue plasters.
- Practical skills. You should show a good range of practical skills in both the preparation and serving of food and beverages. You should also include evidence of good customer care and show that you have worked well during the event.
- Organisational skills. Provide evidence in your write-up of the event that you were able to work to your time plan and that you used the correct equipment and used resources well during the event.

Remember to include photographs of your event and how you worked, as it helps the moderator when they are assessing your work.

In order for you to access the higher range of marks for this section you should:

- use equipment and tools competently
- show a wide range of skills and processes when making the dishes
- work hygienically and safely
- organise work in a logical way
- complete tasks in the allotted time
- carry out planned work independently
- demonstrate a high level of quality to ensure a successful event.

Evaluating the task (25 marks)

When you have completed the event you should analyse and evaluate the event and include evidence of the following:

- Time management. You should evaluate how you managed to work to the time plan on the day of the event and how you kept up with the work when planning the event.
- Standard of personal presentation. Describe how you worked during the trialling of the foods and during the event itself.
- Safe and hygienic practices. Discuss and evaluate how you worked safely and hygienically at all times. Include examples.
- Skills. Describe the skills you have learned while holding the event and which skills you need to develop further.
- Costing. Did you manage to work within your original budget? If not describe why. How much profit did you make? Show how this is worked out.
- Customer satisfaction. Include evidence of customer satisfaction and feedback. Have they filled out an evaluation form for the event? Did you receive any thank you letters? Have you had a written account put in the school/college magazine?
- Success. How do you know your event was successful? Describe the things that went well and remember to include teamwork in your evaluation.
- Improvements. If you were to do the event again, what would you change, and why?

Your evaluation should be detailed and include all areas of your event. You need to include an evaluation of your research and planning, not just an evaluation of how the event went on the day.

In order for you to access the higher range of marks for this section you should:

- produce a full evaluation of the event
- include a realistic evaluation of the time allocations
- suggest areas for improvement
- write clearly, with few errors
- use specialist vocabulary.

The evidence for each section should not exceed 15 pages of A4 (or equivalent).

Just a note to thank you and all the staff for making Saturday a great evening.

As always, everyone at the restaurant was really helpful and friendly.

The food was fantastic – special thanks to the catering team.

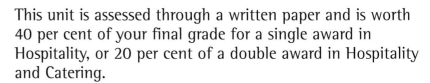

This unit is assessed through a written paper and is worth 40 per cent of your final grade for a single award in Hospitality, or 20 per cent of a double award in Hospitality and Catering.

The paper lasts for 1¼ hours and will have a range of questions covering all the areas you have learned throughout the course and through carrying out your event. The start of the paper will be assessed through recall of knowledge. The questions towards the middle and end of the paper will ask for more detail and explanation of your answers. Some examples of questions and answers are set out in Chapter 5.

In order to gain full marks for the longer questions, you should always answer the question by giving relevant facts, reasons and examples.

Examples of questions and answers

This section gives some examples of the kinds of questions you will have to answer in your written exam. It is always a good idea to try several past questions so that you can see how the questions are set out and what kind of responses you are expected to give. By doing this you increase your chances of getting a good mark.

This section in two parts:

- Part 1 gives two long questions, one for Hospitality and one for Catering, each with a candidate's example answers. Mark schemes are provided at the end of each question.
- Part 2 gives a set of shorter example questions, with the number of marks available shown in brackets after each one. A detailed mark scheme for the questions is given at the end of the section.

Remember that the Catering examination will also be available as an electronic assessment. Practice examples can be found on the WJEC website.

Mark schemes

The mark schemes show what the examiner will expect you to say in your answers. They are broken down into sections, and show how many marks are possible for a list, a simple answer and a detailed, clear answer.

ACTIVITY

Have a look at Questions 1 and 2 and the answers that the candidate gave.

Can you think of anything that is missing? How would you have answered the question?

Read through the relevant sections of the book to help you. Have a go *before* you look at the mark scheme.

REMEMBER

Remember that the questions that come later in the exam paper require long and detailed answers, not just a list. It is a good idea to highlight key words in longer questions to help you to focus when you are writing your answer.

ACTIVITY

Try to work out how many marks you think the candidate would get for each part of their answer, and give your reasons why.

Part 1

The answers to Questions 1 and 2 (below) did not gain full marks. However, they are classed as good responses.

Question 1

Elen and Troy are opening a new restaurant in a large city. They want to target the young professionals who work in the city, as well as the visiting tourists. They plan to serve food from 11 a.m. until 9 p.m.

They want a modern restaurant with a semi open-plan kitchen, which will be visible to the customers. Customers will be able to see their dishes being freshly and quickly prepared.

a) Discuss the main points to consider when planning the choice of foods for the menu. (6)

CANDIDATE'S ANSWER

When Elen and Troy open their new restaurant their menu needs to be carefully planned to ensure that they reach the needs of their target customers 'young professionals who work in the city'. The design and layout of the menu needs to be accurate to appeal to these customers. The choice of dishes served needs to vary from meat to vegetarians. Meals such as 'burger and chips' could be sold, but altered to ensure that they are healthy. The restaurant should supply both à la carte and table d'hôte menus as younger customers may prefer a set price menu which is easy and affordable. Lunchtime meals such as toasted panini served with chips, or scampi and chips would be an easy but effective dish to sell. Dietary needs need to be taken into consideration, so customers who suffer from a nut allergy or wheat allergy need to be taken into consideration. Also people of different ethnic minorities such as Asian or Chinese need a choice of meal to choose from, so noodles or chicken tikka masala could be dishes to take into consideration.

b) Assess the importance of a well-planned kitchen. (10)

> **CANDIDATE'S ANSWER**
>
> It is important that the layout of the kitchen is well planned for a number of different reasons. If Elen and Troy want a semi-open kitchen in which their customers can see their dishes being cooked and prepared, they need to make sure that there is good organisation and that the appliances are kept clean at all times and are easy to access. Appliances need to be accurately laid out, for example the washing up area would not be good planned near where food is being prepared as this would give the wrong impression to the customer as it would look like poor health and hygiene. Although the kitchen needs to be equipped with most large industrial size appliances, they need to be kept to a minimum to ensure that the kitchen looks presentable and clutter free. The kitchen needs to be accessible to members of staff, so doorways and fire exits must be kept clear. Delivery points need to always be taken into consideration when planning the kitchen. Elen and Troy want their customers to see their food being cooked so an industrial hob needs to be fitted accurately not too close to the customers as it would be a health risk. The right safety equipment needs to be fitted into the kitchen, e.g. fire extinguishers and fire blankets so it meets the expectations of the EHO.

c) Elen and Troy need staff to work in both the food preparation and service area of the restaurant. Discuss the qualities and skills staff will need to be employed in this type of open-plan restaurant.

> **CANDIDATE'S ANSWER**
>
> If Elen and Troy want their staff to work in both food preparation and service their employees will need to be equipped with a number of different skills, the first one being good communication and social skills. They will need to be able to take directions from fellow chefs within the kitchen, but also be able to approach and communicate with their customers in the restaurant. The second skill which will be required is good knowledge of health and hygiene because if they are walking to and from the kitchen they could pick up and spread a large amount of bacteria. Things such as hair tied back and regular washing of hands must be kept to strictly to ensure that there is no contamination of food. Employees must also be conscious of their surroundings as most of the time they will probably be in a rush to meet the customers' needs, so they need to be aware of wet floors, etc. and get them labelled. Employees need to have skills in all areas of the restaurant and need to know how to operate all the technology and appliances such as the till or electric hobs. They need a good sense of time keeping and need to know when each dish is ready to be served as customers can see and will be waiting for their meals to be cooked. If an employee knows that there is an expected

delivery they need to ensure that this is collected and stored in a fast manner so it does not disturb people's meals. Members of staff need to be able to work a kitchen and service rota so there is no confusion about where they are working on that day. They also need to be aware of the Health and Safety at Work Act and that the policy is up to date. Members of staff need to be calm under pressure as a restaurant in a city will get very busy.

Mark scheme for Question 1

a) Answer could include:

- Nutritionally balanced diet.
- Variety of colour, flavour and texture.
- Foods in season.
- Time of year.
- Skills of chef.
- Type of outlet.
- Cost.
- Suitability and appeal to client.
- Time available.
- Latest food trends.

Award 5–6 marks for an answer that recalls detailed knowledge and demonstrates a comprehensive and detailed understanding of menu planning. The answer will include a wide range of points with evidence of detailed discussion. The response is well structured and clearly expressed with few errors.

Award 3–4 marks for an answer that recalls knowledge and demonstrates understanding of menu planning. The answer will include a range of points with evidence of discussion. Expression is adequate to convey meaning but some errors may be apparent.

Award 1–2 marks for an answer that recalls some knowledge and demonstrates a basic knowledge of menu planning. The answer may be a simple list or restricted number of suggestions. Communication will tend to be impeded by poor expression.

b) Answer could include:

- Layout.
- Lighting.
- Materials used.
- Size and extent of the menu it serves.

- Services – gas, electricity, water.
- Amount of capital.
- Types of equipment available.
- Amount of time to be spent using the kitchen.
- The golden triangle: fridge, cooker, sink.
- Separate areas for preparation.
- Hygiene and Food Safety Act.
- Hand-washing facilities.

Award **7–10** marks for an answer that recalls detailed knowledge and demonstrates a comprehensive and detailed understanding of kitchen planning. The answer will include a wide range of points with evidence of detailed discussion. The response is well structured and clearly expressed with few errors.

Award **4–6** marks for an answer that recalls knowledge and demonstrates understanding of kitchen planning. The answer will include a range of points with evidence of discussion. Expression is adequate to convey meaning but some errors may be apparent.

Award **1–3** marks for an answer that recalls some knowledge and demonstrates a basic knowledge of kitchen planning. The answer may be a simple list or restricted number of suggestions. Communication will tend to be impeded by poor expression.

c) Answer could include:

- Good customer skills.
- Team member.
- Excellent communication skills.
- Qualifications in Hospitality and Catering.
- Clean.
- Smart appearance.
- Friendly.
- Knowledge and Certificate in Hygiene.
- Knowledge of special diets.

Award **7–10** marks for an answer that recalls detailed knowledge and demonstrates a comprehensive and detailed understanding of qualities and skills required. The answer will include a wide range of points with evidence of detailed discussion. The response is well structured and clearly expressed with few errors.

Award **4–6** marks for an answer that recalls knowledge and demonstrates understanding of qualities and skills required. The answer will include a range of points with evidence of discussion. Expression is adequate to convey meaning but some errors may be apparent.

Award 1–3 marks for an answer that recalls some knowledge and demonstrates a basic knowledge of qualities and skills required. The answer may be a simple list or restricted number of suggestions. Communication will tend to be impeded by poor expression.

Question 2

Following recent government guidelines, fast food outlets are offering a more varied choice on their menus.

a) State three reasons why we should have a healthy diet. (3)

> **CANDIDATE'S ANSWER**
>
> i) Reduce the risk of obesity in children and young people.
> ii) Keep the body functioning properly, e.g. keeping eyes strong.
> iii) Lower the risk of heart diseases as we get older.

b) Explain how fast food outlets can make their food interesting and healthy to attract more customers. (6)

> **CANDIDATE'S ANSWER**
>
> Healthy food means having a balance of protein, fat and carbohydrates. Fast food outlets can provide this but they need to advertise well to sell. For younger children they can create a cartoon animal to set an example by eating the healthy foods. If children see bright colourful characters eating foods they will want to follow. Often famous people are used to attract teenagers and adults. The food can be made more interesting by adding new flavours and dressings. More colour and variety in foods. For example rather than beef burgers make minted lamb burgers or pork and apple burgers. Offer a range of dressings or sauces, salads and cheeses. Also they must create a more vegetarian friendly menu using meat alternatives, beans, peas and lentils to attract more vegetarian customers. They then have to advertise well to inform people of the new menu available.

c) Suggest ways in which a burger bar could offer alternatives for vegetarians that are both healthy and tasty. (6)

CANDIDATE'S ANSWER

A burger bar can adapt the products it sells to suit vegetarian needs easily. They can provide 'veggie' burgers as many already do but they can also introduce meat alternatives such as tofu, soya and quorn. These are all suitable alternatives for vegetarians. Also they could offer lentils, peas and beans in soups or stews. The burger vans also need to consider vegans who do not eat any dairy products either. This means they cannot offer cheese or milk in two or more products to make them suitable for vegans. As vegetarians do not eat meat it is important they get protein and other essential food groups from the foods they eat. This is why lentils and beans are good. They are high in protein and provide a great source for an alternative menu. If the burger bar wanted to expand more they could offer salads and seafood options.

Mark scheme for Question 2

a) Any three of the following:

- prevent heart disease
- prevent obesity
- reduces high levels of cholesterol
- minimise risk of high blood pressure
- prevent tooth decay
- live longer, more active lifestyle.

1 mark for each correct answer.

b) Methods of cooking, grilling instead of frying:

- offer low fat alternatives
- use less processed food
- offer healthy drinks, yoghurt or milk based, flavoured water
- offer interesting salads and vegetable dishes
- wraps instead of burgers
- sweeteners instead of sugar
- healthy choices for kids, e.g. vegetable sticks and fruit
- add herbs and spices instead of salt
- promotional offers on new products such as wraps
- low-fat dressings on salads.

Award 1–2 marks for an answer that recalls some knowledge and demonstrates a basic knowledge of how to make foods healthier. The answer may be a simple list or restricted number of suggestions. Communication will tend to be impeded by poor expression.

Award 3–4 marks for an answer that recalls knowledge and demonstrates understanding of how to make foods healthier. The answer will include a range of points with evidence of discussion. Expression is adequate to convey meaning but some errors may be apparent.

Award 5–6 marks for an answer that recalls detailed knowledge and demonstrates a comprehensive and detailed understanding of how to make foods healthier. The answer will include a wide range of points with evidence of detailed discussion. The response is well structured and clearly expressed with few errors.

c) Use of quorn, tofu, veggie burgers, wraps. Added flavour with spices and herbs or by adding a sauce to the product.

Award 1–2 marks for an answer that recalls some knowledge and demonstrates a basic knowledge of how to make vegetarian alternatives. The answer may be a simple list or restricted number of suggestions. Communication will tend to be impeded by poor expression.

Award 3–4 marks for an answer that recalls knowledge and demonstrates understanding of how to make vegetarian alternatives. The answer will include a range of points with evidence of discussion. Expression is adequate to convey meaning but some errors may be apparent.

Award 5–6 marks for an answer that recalls detailed knowledge and demonstrates a comprehensive and detailed understanding of how to make vegetarian alternatives. The answer will include a wide range of points with evidence of detailed discussion. The response is well structured and clearly expressed with few errors.

Part 2

Try to answer the following questions. The amount of marks for each question is given in brackets. Have a go before you look at the mark scheme. When you have completed the answer, check the mark scheme to see what you may have missed and how the marks are given.

1. You are working for a firm of Contract Caterers who have been asked to prepare and serve a meal for an engagement party.
   a) What do you understand by the term contract caterers? (2)
   b) Hazard Analysis and Critical Control Points are important when preparing and serving food for the occasion.

Identify and explain **four** safety checks that are critical to the safe preparation and serving of food. (4)

2. A catering firm is planning to offer a party service for children.
   a) Plan a suitable menu including **two** savoury dishes, **one** sweet dish and a drink. (4)
   b) Discuss points the catering firm must consider when planning a suitable party menu. (6)
   c) Describe how the caterer could make the table and room look attractive for the party. (3)

3. a) Describe the qualities and/or skills needed by a head chef in a large restaurant. (4)
   b) Discuss the role the restaurant manager has in the running of the hotel restaurant. (4)

4. Record keeping is important and helps to ensure the smooth running of the hotel industry.
   a) Explain why the following types of record keeping are used in the reception area of a hotel. (5)
      i) Room lists
      ii) Booking forms
      iii) Customer telephone bills
      iv) Customer survey
      v) Restaurant orders.
   b) Explain why stock control records are used in the kitchen. (3)

5. Jacky and Nicky have recently taken over a busy country pub specialising in evening meals and Sunday lunches. They intend to refurbish the kitchen area as it is badly planned making it unhygienic and difficult to work in.
   a) Discuss the factors which influence the planning and design of the new kitchen area. (4)
   b) Before the kitchen can be used the local EHO will make a visit. Explain the role of the EHO within the kitchen area. (4)
   c) What advice could the EHO give Jacky and Nicky on the training of staff for their new kitchen? (2)

Mark scheme for Part 2

1. a) Award **1** mark for simple list or single comment that reflects some knowledge of the role of contract caterer.

   Award **2** marks for answer which lists one or more of the above or is descriptive in content.

The role of contract caterer could include the following points:

- Has overall responsibility for organisation of event working to information given by the customer.
- Complete all administration for food for the event including ordering food, arranging the chef to cook the meal beforehand.
- Arranging the wait staff to serve the food on the day, these could be agency staff so the contract caterer would have to liaise with the agency.
- Organise along with the customer where the event will be held, liaise with the manager at the venue.
- Organise table layouts for service.
- Set the standards for service.
- Co-operate with chef in menu planning.
- Liaise with the customer throughout the planning of the event and ensure that the customer's wishes are met fully.
- Hold meeting before service to ensure smooth running of meal and solve any problems that may occur.

b) **1 mark** for four points with no detail for reasons or if they only refer to one safety check, e.g. personal hygiene or risk assessment.

2–3 marks for list that shows some knowledge and understanding of HACCP and how to prevent with little description.

4 marks for a well written answer that reflects the knowledge and understanding of HACCP with detailed description of all relevant areas with clear explanation. For full marks they should correctly identify temperature zones.

Answer could include:

- Checks on purchase of goods, dates and quality – to ensure food is safe to eat.
- Safe storage of food before, during and after preparation with temperature of fridges, etc.
- Use of different chopping boards, knives, etc. – colours as examples could be given, therefore avoiding cross contamination.
- Cooling of prepared foods, rapidly to 1–4°C – to prevent bacterial growth.

- Use of blast chillers to cool food rapidly – to prevent bacterial growth.
- Checking temperature of fridges/freezers.
- Checking core temperature of cooked meats 72°C – to ensure they are working correctly.
- Personal hygiene (only allow one, e.g. hands washed, whites worn).
- Safe reheating of foods to core temperature of 72°C – use of temperature probe.
- Minimal time in danger zone. Food served quickly. 37–63°C.

2. a) Allow 1 mark for **each** suitable item.

Savoury – named sandwiches, dips, pizzas, pastry dish, fast food option. (Must include a protein food), pasta option, jacket potato option, sausages, curry and rice.

Sweet – mousse, fruit jelly, fresh fruit salad, trifle, biscuits, gateau, ice cream, named cakes, jam tarts.

Drink – smoothies, milkshakes, fruit juices, fizzy drinks, **no** alcohol.

b) Possible points discussed.

Point	Discussion
Food costs	Bulk buying will help reduce production cost.
Where food is to be served	Location of venue, facilities for storing dishes at correct temperature.
How the food is to be served	Buffet, plate service, wait service, seating arrangements, portion size.
Age of the children	Menu must be appropriate to the age group. Likes and dislikes.
Kitchen facilities	It is possible to assemble some dishes on site. Number of fridges, is there a freezer? Oven for hot food.
Operating costs	Must include labour costs, wear and tear of equipment, fuel, travelling, number to cater for.
Season	Hot or cold food. Using food in season helps reduce food costs.
Contrast in flavour, texture and appearance	A variety will provide a more balanced meal and make food more interesting and appetising. Nutritional balance
Special diet	Vegetarian/allergy/cultural needs

Allow **1–2 marks** for basic principles discussed. Possible reference made to only 1 or 2 of the above points, bullet points only. Answer may resemble a list with no discussion.

Allow **3–4 marks** for answers where candidates will have discussed any of the above points. Some understanding of menu planning evident.

Allow **5–6 marks** for a very good answer. Candidates will have discussed most of the above points. Showing a good understanding of menu planning.

c) Allow up to 3 marks for any suitable suggestions on how to make table/room attractive.

Answers could include:

- Seating arrangements/place names. Size of chairs/tables.
- Toys/games/activities.
- Balloons/banners/hats/poppers/posters.
- Lighting, i.e. Halloween.
- Themes, e.g. Thomas the Tank Engine.
- Paper table cloths, colourful cups, plates (plastic/paper).
- Party bags.
- Music.
- Birthday cards/presents displayed.
- Decorations must be specific.

3. a) Answers should include:

- The chef should have the relevant qualifications – City and Guilds, BTec, in-house or any professional training as it identifies the knowledge of the chef.
- Should have knowledge of a range of recipes developed from experience.
- Should be able to work well under pressure.
- Should have a good palate to know what foods go well together.
- Be able to produce meals with limited ingredients in case food orders do not arrive.
- Should have knowledge of stock control as they are responsible for the budget and costing and are responsible to the manager to make a profit.
- Should have knowledge and qualifications in food safety and hygiene.

- Should be a team leader, have clear leadership skills, have good communication skills and relate well to others as they are responsible for the staff.

Award 1–2 marks for an answer that reflects some knowledge and a basic understanding of the qualities of a good head chef. The answer may just resemble a list. 1 mark only for repetition or limited answer.

Award 3–4 marks for a well written answer that reflects knowledge and understanding of the qualities and skills required to be a good head chef. Reasons should be given.

b) Answer could include the following:

- Has overall responsibility for the organisation of the restaurant and solves any problems which may arise.
- Sets the standards for service within the restaurant.
- Complete all administration for food and beverage service areas.
- Organises banquets and functions.
- Organises table layouts for service.
- Solves any problems with staff rotas, holidays, etc.
- Organises training for staff.
- Completes duty rotas and holiday lists.
- Holds meetings to ensure the smooth running of areas and service.
- Co-operates with the chef when planning menus.
- Updates wine lists.
- Liaises with wine waiters.
- Liaise with staff and informs them when foods are running low or no longer available.
- Liaise with reception/booking desk to ensure restaurant is not overbooked for service.
- Takes bookings for meals.

Award 1–2 marks for an answer that recalls some knowledge and demonstrates a basic knowledge of the role of restaurant manager. The answer may be a simple list or restricted number of suggestions. Communication will tend to be impeded by poor expression.

Award 3–4 marks for an answer that recalls knowledge and demonstrates understanding of the role of restaurant manager. The answer may relate to a limited number of points with evidence of discussion. Expression is adequate to convey meaning but some errors may be apparent. They may discuss one area in detail and only list other areas

Award 5–6 marks for an answer that recalls detailed knowledge and demonstrates a comprehensive and detailed understanding of the role of restaurant manager. The answer will include a wide range of points with evidence of detailed discussion. The response is well structured and clearly expressed with few errors.

Do not credit answers where discussion relates to hotel manager or chef.

4. 1 mark for each detailed correct answer.

i) This enables the receptionist to pass the information on to the housekeeper and she can then check the rooms are ready for use. The housekeeper will also know which rooms are becoming vacant and need cleaning each day. It also enables the receptionist to allocate any rooms available to customers.

ii) The receptionist will know what rooms and function rooms are available for hire and when. They will have this information to hand when dealing with enquiries on the phone. This helps with the smooth running of the hotel.

iii) This allows the customers' bills to be made up ready for when they check out. Itemised bills ensure the customer knows what they are being charged for and when calls were made.

iv) A customer survey helps the Hotel/Restaurant to make sure they do the best they can. Customer feedback is a good way of finding out what the customer wants and how service can be improved. Any problems that may have occurred will be highlighted by the customer.

v) This enables the receptionist to work out the customer's bill, by telling them what food the customer has eaten and how much it costs. It also enables the restaurant manager to check the correct foods have been served. This can be cross referenced with the kitchen copy to check on meals served and stock held.

b) Stock Control records are used in the kitchen so that the chefs can see at a glance what stock needs to be ordered to produce the meals and what stock is held in the store.

Food stuffs are often signed out when used so the Head Chef can see at a glance what stock is used more frequently.

It enables the Chef to see the dates the goods arrived and ensure they are used within the dates on the item.

Old stock is brought forward and used first. New stock is put to the back and used last.

Foods are signed for when delivered and have been checked for dates and damage. This is shown on the stock records.

Damaged stock is not acceptable, this is recorded on the stock sheets so the Chef knows that item is not available.

Only foods that can be made from the stock available will be on the menu.

Stock can be checked regularly and new orders made, this will mean that perishable stock is limited and used as quickly as possible.

Walk-in fridges and freezers often have the stock list on the door so you can see at a glance what stock is available.

3 marks for clear, well written and detailed answer that reflects knowledge and understanding of stock control records and their use. The suggestions should be logical and practical.

1–2 marks for answer that covers relevant points with some brief reasons given.

1 mark for outline answer with no explanation. Or answer that is just a list. Or answer that covers only one point but in detail.

5. **a)** Answer should include:

- Ergonomic features required for a safe and healthy working environment.
- Layout.

- Lighting.
- Heating.
- Services available – gas, electric, water.
- Skill level of chef – what equipment can he use safely.
- Amount of expenditure, costs.
- Type of equipment available.
- Hygiene and Food Safety Act.
- Design and décor.
- Size and extent of menu and market it serves.
- Storage area for food.
- Environmental considerations – how can they reduce, reuse, recycle.

4 marks for clear, well written and detailed answer that reflects knowledge and understanding of planning and design of new kitchen area. The suggestions should be logical and practical.

2–3 marks for answer that covers relevant points with some brief reasons given.

1 mark for outline answer with no explanation.

b) Answers should include:

- To check if the new facilities are up to standard.
- Checking on hygiene procedures.
- To look at food storage areas.
- Fridge temperatures.
- Check for pest infestation.
- Check food is fit for sale.
- Check hand washing facilities are available.
- Temperature of cooked foods.
- Correct storage of foods.
- Dates on foods.

4 marks for clear well written and detailed answer that reflects knowledge and understanding of the role of EHO. The suggestions should be logical and practical.

2–3 marks for answer that covers relevant points with some brief reasons given.

1 mark for outline answer with no explanation.

c) Answers should include:

- Give verbal advice on how to keep premises clean and hygienic.

- Advice on the Basic Hygiene Certificate.
- Training sessions for staff.
- Leaflets can be given on safe food practice.
- Advice given on illness and when staff cannot work with food.

1 mark for 1 simple answer.

2 marks for detailed answer with clear explanation.

Questions often require specific knowledge and understanding. Candidates may be asked to:

Define: give the meaning of ...

List: make a list.

State: write clearly but briefly.

Describe: give an account of ...

Discuss: give important aspects of ...

give advantages and disadvantages of ...

Explain: make clear, giving reasons.

Evaluate: give important aspects of ...
give your own opinion of ...

Note:
- The questions at the end of the papers will need a high level of understanding and candidates will be expected to discuss, explain or evaluate their answers. These questions are often criteria marked.
- Answering questions in 'bullet points' is popular with candidates *but* often counts as 'writing a list'. Candidates answering questions in this way will not earn good marks for criteria marked questions.

Common errors

Candidates misread questions or see 'key' words and assume they know what the question is about. Examples include:

Fast food – often misinterpreted as 'junk' food, instead of good quality food with fast service.

Food safety – often wrongly considered to be preventing accidents rather than good food hygiene.

Commodities – often wrongly considered to be equipment rather than food.

Tips for candidates

Read each question thoroughly.

Underline key words so you know what the question is asking.

For the essay type questions at the end of the papers, draw up a short plan before starting or highlight key words to help you answer the question.

Look at the number of marks available for the question and write enough to earn the marks.

The exam is not a race – there are no prizes for finishing first.

GOOD LUCK!

Glossary

abdominal pain: pain in the stomach area.

accommodation services: the housekeeping side of an establishment.

accompaniments: items offered separately to main dish.

à la carte: separately priced menu, from which items are prepared and cooked to order.

al dente: firm to the bite.

allergic reaction: way in which the body responds to some foods (for example, a rash, swelling or anaphylactic shock).

allergy: an adverse reaction by the body to certain substances (including foods).

attitude: the way in which you approach customers.

appearance: the way you look to customers. It is important to look clean and smart.

au gratin: sprinkled with cheese or breadcrumbs and browned.

bain-marie: container of water to keep foods hot without fear of burning.

BHA: British Hospitality Association.

BII: British Institute of Inn-Keeping.

binary fission: how bacteria multiply by dividing in two.

brûlée: burned cream.

body language: the way in which your body reflects your mood.

bouquet garni: small bundle of herbs.

chefs: staff who are responsible for preparing and cooking food safely and hygienically.

CIEH: Chartered Institute of Environmental Health.

coeliac disease: a serious gluten intolerance. A person with this condition must avoid all forms of wheat, including wholemeal, whole wheat and wheat meal flour, bran, pasta, noodles, semolina, bread, pastry, sauces thickened with flour, muesli, wheat, rye, barley and oat breakfast cereals, beer, and other malted drinks.

complaint: expression of dissatisfaction.

contaminated: containing an additional substance that should not be there.

contract caterers: people who prepare the food for functions such as weddings, banquets, garden parties and parties in private houses. They may prepare and cook the food in advance and deliver it to the venue, or they may cook it on site. They may also provide staff to serve the food if required.

core temperature: temperature in the middle of the food.

corporate: group or chain of businesses. Can be shared, as in uniform or identity.

coulis: sauce made of fruit or vegetable puree.

covers: number of customers.

criteria: the standards and limits judged to be right.

croutons: cubes of bread that are fried or grilled.

customer: a person who buys or uses the products and services.

customer care: how well you look after the paying guests.

décor: how the room is set up and decorated.

diarrhoea: 'the runs'.

EHO: Environmental Health Officer.

en croute: in pastry.

entrée: main course.

evaluation: the assessment of performance.

feedback: information given in response.

fever: a raised temperature.

flambé: cook with flame by burning away the alcohol.

food and drink service: serving area in a restaurant, café or bar.

food hygiene: practices that make sure that food is safe to eat.

food intolerance: condition obliging someone to avoid a certain food because of the effect on their body (e.g. a person with lactose intolerance must avoid milk products).

food poisoning: an illness caught from eating contaminated food.

front-of-house: reception area of an establishment.

garnish: trimming served with the main item.

greeting and seating: how the customers are met and shown to their table.

HACCP: Hazard analysis and critical control points. Stages used in food production to ensure food is safe to eat.

HCIMA: Hotel and Catering International Management Association (now known as the Institute of Hospitality).

High-risk foods: food that provides the perfect conditions for the growth and reproduction of micro-organisms that contaminate the food and make it unsafe to eat.

hospitality and catering industry: businesses that provide food, drink and/or accommodation.

identify: recognise, discover.

industry: business or trade.

in-house: on the premises.

julienne: strips of vegetables cut to matchstick size.

lactose intolerance: condition obliging someone to avoid milk, cheese, butter, yoghurt and processed foods that contain milk products.

legislation: laws made and enforced to protect customers.

logo: a printed symbol or trademark used by a company as its emblem.

management: people who are in charge of specific areas.

manner: the way you speak to customers.

marinade: richly spiced liquid used to give flavour and assist in tenderising meat and fish.

mise en place: basic preparation prior to assembling products.

nausea: feeling of sickness.

nutrients: substances found in foods that help us grow and resist infection.

overheads: items a business must pay for before it makes a profit, including materials, workforce, transport and energy.

People 1st: Sector skills council for hospitality, leisure and travel and tourism.

perishable: does not keep well.

personal hygiene: good personal hygiene ensures that germs found in or on the body do not transfer to food.

planning: preparations or arrangements done beforehand.

policies: course of action in place that determines rules (e.g. to enable a safe working environment).

portion control: method used to limit the amount of food a customer is given to the same each time.

promotion: advertising a business to get more trade.

protective: shielding, making safe.

purée: smooth mixture made from food passed through a sieve.

quality: a measure of the level of excellence or standard of a product or service.

quality assurance: a promise or guarantee that services and products are of a particular standard.
quality control: method used to ensure the quality is maintained throughout all stages of making.

reduce: concentrate a liquid by boiling.
regulations: legal requirements.
research: looking at existing products.
response: how you react verbally and in your body language.
review: look back on something and see how it was dealt with.
RIPH: Royal Institute of Public Health.
risk assessment: ways of identifying and preventing accidents.
roux: thickening of cooked flour and fat.
RSPH: Royal Society for the Promotion of Health.

sauce: a liquid that has been thickened.
sauté: tossed in fat.
seating plan: plan of who will be sitting where, on what table.
skill: the ability to carry out something.
SSC: Sector Skills Council.

table d'hôte: menu with fixed courses and limited choice.
time-plan: a logical and ordered plan for a product or event, from start to finish.

wait staff: waiters and waitresses.
wholegrain: using the whole of the grain of wheat.

venue: place where an event is held.
vomiting: being sick.

Index

Index

Index

Index